Peugeot 404 1960-75 Autobook

By Kenneth Ball

and the Autobooks Team of Technical Writers

Peugeot 404, 1618cc, 1960-75

Autobooks

Autobooks Ltd. Golden Lane Brighton BN1 2QJ England

The AUTOBOOK series of Workshop Manuals is the largest in the world and covers the majority of British and Continental motor cars, as well as all major Japanese and Australian models. For a full list see the back of this manual.

**This book is to be returned on or before
the last date stamped below.**

LEARNING FOR LIFE
LONDON BOROUGH OF SUTTON LIBRARIES

RENEWALS   Please quote: date of return, your ticket number
and computer label number for each item.

CONTENTS

Introduction

Acknowledgement

ISBN 0 85147 591 4

First Edition   1970
Reprinted   1970
Second Edition, fully revised   1972
Reprinted   1973
Third Edition, fully revised   1973
Fourth Edition, fully revised   1974
Fifth Edition, fully revised   1975

995

Printed and bound in Brighton England for Autobooks Ltd by G. Beard & Son Ltd   C

ACKNOWLEDGEMENT

We wish to thank Peugeot Ltd for their co-operation and also for supplying data and illustrations. Considerable assistance has also been given by owners, who have discussed their cars in detail, and we would like to express our gratitude for this invaluable advice and help.

INTRODUCTION

This do-it-yourself Workshop Manual has been specially written for the owner who wishes to maintain his car in first class condition and to carry out his own servicing and repairs. Considerable savings on garage charges can be made, and one can drive in safety and confidence knowing the work has been done properly.

Comprehensive step-by-step instructions and illustrations are given on all dismantling, overhauling and assembling operations. Certain assemblies require the use of expensive special tools, the purchase of which would be unjustified. In these cases information is included but the reader is recommended to hand the unit to the agent for attention.

Throughout the Manual hints and tips are included which will be found invaluable, and there is an easy to follow fault diagnosis at the end of each chapter.

Whilst every care has been taken to ensure correctness of information it is obviously not possible to guarantee complete freedom from errors or to accept liability arising from such errors or omissions.

Instructions may refer to the righthand or lefthand sides of the vehicle or the components. These are the same as the righthand or lefthand of an observer standing behind the car and looking forward.

CHAPTER 1

THE ENGINE

1:1 Description

The engine used in the Peugeot 404 is a four cylinder in-line, water-cooled unit with overhead valves operated by pushrods from a side mounted camshaft, which is chain driven from the crankshaft sprocket.

Cubic capacity is 1618cc obtained from a bore and stroke of 84 mm and 73 mm respectively. The type number was XC when introduced but with periodic modification this became type XC7 in 1970.

All engines have wet cylinder liners made of centrifugal cast iron and a light alloy 'alpax type' cylinder head with offset spherical cap-shaped combustion chambers. The valve guides and seats are made of special cast iron and are removable.

The valves are made of chromium nickel steel with a hard chrome plating on their bearing lengths. Each valve is held by an inner and outer spring which are identical for inlet or exhaust valves.

The forged steel crankshaft rests on three main bearings in the XC engines, and on five main bearings in the XC5 and later engines. The longitudinal play is limited by two thrust flanges on either side of the rear main bearing.

All models are equipped with an electro-magnetic cooling fan that disconnects itself automatically when the water temperature is low. The fan cuts itself out when the temperature drops to 68°C and cuts in again at 82°C.

The carburetter is a Solex 32 PBICA on all XC engines and early XC5 engines with a Solex 34 PBICA on later XC5 installations.

The drive from the engine is transmitted through a single dry plate clutch. The clutch thrust bearing is made of graphite and must be lubricated every 1900 miles with 1 cc of engine oil.

When fitted into the car the engine is tilted at an angle of 45 deg. to the right. At the same time it slants downwards at the rear to lower the drive line. This in turn lowers the bonnet line and the centre of gravity. To the owner it has the great advantage of bringing all the engine accessories, the carburetter, generator, distributor and fuel pump onto the 'up' side of the engine making them all easily accessible. The one exception is the spark plugs which are somewhat shrouded.

1:2 Working on engine in car

If the owner is not a skilled automobile engineer it is suggested that before starting work he should read the 'Hints on Maintenance and Overhaul' to be found at the end of this manual. The need for cleanliness must be stressed and the operator will save himself much time

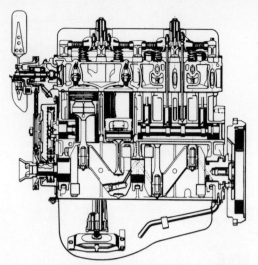

FIG 1:1   Sectioned view of the XC engine

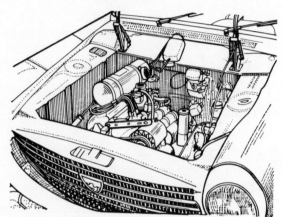

FIG 1:2   View of engine with bonnet removed

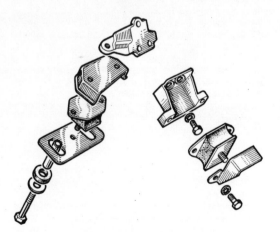

FIG 1:3   Exploded view of engine front mounts

and trouble by carrying out operations in an orderly manner, and by marking each part before dismantling to facilitate easier reassembly. Always use the approved grades of lubricant.

The operations of removing the water pump, distributor, carburetter, cylinder head, clutch and transmission and the adjustment of the timing chain can all be carried out without removing the engine from the car.

For working underneath the car it is often helpful to have the car raised on jacks or blocks. **Any supports must be firmly based and not likely to collapse or serious injury could result.**

1:3 Removing the engine

Before starting to disconnect the engine drain the cooling system. If antifreeze has been used collect the coolant in a clean container and save for refilling on completion.

Disconnect and remove the engine in the following manner:

1 Disconnect the battery.
2 Remove the windshield washer jets, the bonnet, the starting handle and the windshield washer reservoir.
3 Remove the carburetter air cleaner, the ignition coil, the battery and the town horn. The engine is now easily accessible and a view of the engine with the bonnet removed is shown in **FIG 1:2**.
4 Disconnect the radiator hoses, the carburetter heating hose and the car heating hoses.
5 Disconnect and remove the radiator and heating system return hose.
6 Remove the two starter to clutch housing attachment screws.
7 Disconnect the choke and accelerator controls.
8 Disconnect the various electrical leads from the engine including the starter, generator, cooling fan switch and pressure switch.
9 Remove the fuel line from the oil breather.
10 Remove the clutch housing coverplates.
11 Remove the two bolts connecting the exhaust pipe to the exhaust manifold.
12 From underneath the car remove the bolt holding the exhaust pipe clamp to the transmission housing.
13 Support the bellhousing and remove the three Allen bolts holding the bellhousing to the engine.
14 Attach hoisting gear to the engine and support the weight of the engine.
15 Remove the nuts from the engine front mounts. An exploded view of the front mounts is shown in **FIG 1:3** and the position of the engine and the front and rear mounts can be seen in **FIG 1:4**. The rear mount is a rubber support which is integral with the body. This holds the gearbox and reduces the effects of torque.
16 Raise the engine slightly and move it forward to free from the transmission. As soon as it is clear, turn the engine diagonally as shown in **FIG 1:5** and lift the engine clear of the body.

1:4 Removing and replacing the cylinder head

In order to avoid misshaping the cylinder head it is essential that it should be removed from a **cold** engine. Disconnect the battery and drain the cooling system, retaining the coolant for further use if antifreeze has been added.

1 Remove the spark plug leads, spark plugs and distributor cap.
2 Remove the top radiator hose, rocker lubrication pipe and the fan belt.
3 Disconnect from the cylinder head the lower radiator hose and the heater connection.
4 Remove the petrol feed and the distributor vacuum lines, disconnect the accelerator and choke controls at the carburetter and remove the air cleaner and the rocker cover.
5 Remove the carburetter and inlet pipe with the diffuser.
6 Unfasten the exhaust flange, the front muffler attachment collar and the sliding lug of the generator to cylinder head.
7 Disconnect the electrical leads to the magnetic fan.
8 Refer to **FIG 1:6** and remove the cylinder head attaching bolts Nos. 8 and 12.
9 Fit cylinder head guides, 8.0115, into the holes vacated by bolts 8 and 12 and screw in completely. The guides have a knurled end fitting with a lefthand thread which should unscrew as soon as the guide comes level with the top of the rocker gear bearing.
10 Remove the remaining cylinder head bolts and rocker attaching nuts and withdraw the rocker assembly and pushrods, cylinder head and gasket.
11 Lock the cylinder liners by means of the locking screws 8.0104D as shown in **FIG 1:7**. If the special screws are not available a large washer may be used in conjunction with a spacer and a cylinder head bolt.

Before replacing the cylinder head carefully clean the joint faces on the cylinder block and the cylinder head. Ensure that both faces are true. The maximum out of true tolerance is .05mm. Should this tolerance be exceeded the cylinder head joint face may be surfaced providing the minimum overall depth of the cylinder head is not reduced below 91.5mm$\pm$.15. The cylinder block joint face should never be machined.

The cylinder head gasket is made of an asbestos sheet set between two sheets of galvanized iron. As from September 1960, the setting width at both ends of the joint has been reduced from 3 to 2mm. In addition, the setting at the rear end has been interrupted, in order to improve the elasticity of the gasket. The corners of the gasket are cut in order to permit measuring with a set of shims the thickness of the gasket under load. Thickness of the gasket under 1500 kg load, equal to normal torque loading of the cylinder head, should be 1.5mm $\pm$.1.

Before placing the gasket on the cylinder block, coat the gasket on both sides with light grease or engine oil.

Replace the cylinder head in the following manner:

1 Remove the cylinder liner locking screws and place the cylinder head gasket in position on the cylinder block. The cylinder head gasket should be fitted with the marking DESSUS facing upwards. **Make sure that the crankshaft is not rotated while the liners are not locked in position with the retaining screws.**
2 Place the cylinder head in position on the cylinder block (see **FIG 1:8**) and fit Nos. 3 and 7 retaining bolts (see **FIG 1:6**). Assemble the pushrods and rocker assembly and fit the remaining cylinder head bolts and

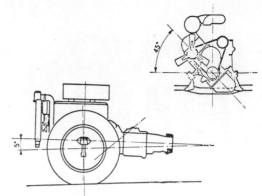

FIG 1:4 Showing the position of the engine mounts and the angular disposition of the engine in the car

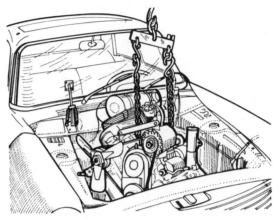

FIG 1:5 Method of slinging the engine

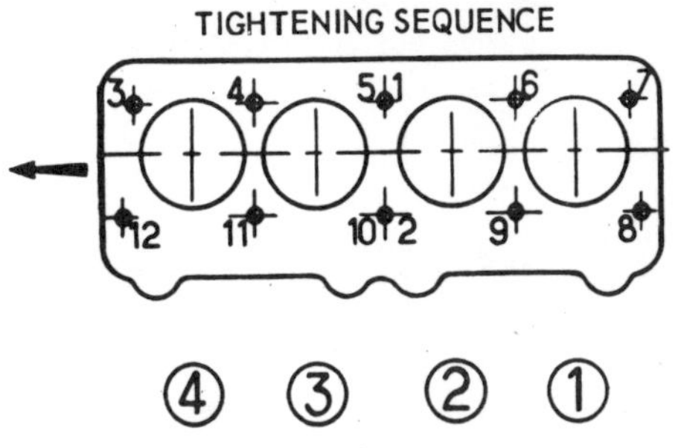

TIGHTENING SEQUENCE

FIG 1:6 Cylinder head bolt tightening sequence. Note that the cylinders are numbered from the rear of the engine

rocker retaining nuts. Remove the guide pins and fit the bolts 8 and 12.
3 Tighten the cylinder head nuts and bolts in two stages in the correct sequence (see **FIG 1:6**), to the following torque:
First tightening   29 lb ft
Final tightening   51 lb ft
4 Install all components and connections by reversing the removal sequence.

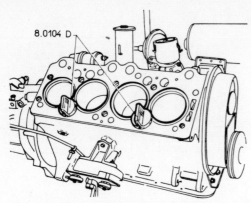

FIG 1:7 Cylinder liners locked with locking screw

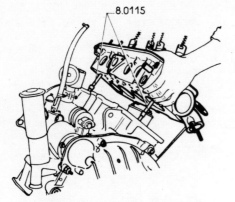

FIG 1:8 Refitting the cylinder head

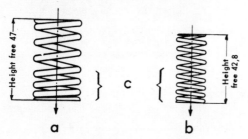

FIG 1:9 Valve spring dimensions

5 Adjust the rocker clearances. After the engine has been run for approximately 100 miles, the cylinder head bolts and nuts should be checked and tightened to the correct torque. The rocker clearances must then be readjusted to the correct figure of 0.10 mm (.004 inch) for Inlet, and 0.25 mm (.010 inch) for Exhaust.

1:5 Servicing the head and valve gear

Remove the cylinder head as in the preceding section. If decarbonizing is intended plug all the waterways in the top face of the cylinder head with pieces of rag. Scrape the carbon from the combustion chamber in the cylinder head before removing the valves to avoid damage to the valve seats.

1 Use a spring compressor and with the springs compressed, remove the valve retainers. Release the compressor and lift off the cap, springs and oil dripper caps on the stems of the valves. Remove the valve after marking it to ensure correct reassembly. Clean the ports free from carbon and examine the valve seats and stems.

2 Valve stems should show no signs of 'picking up' or wear, neither should they be bent. Regrind the valve seats with grinding paste if the seats are not too deeply pitted. A refaced valve should be renewed if the bearing of the valve upon its seat is less than 1.5mm in width.

3 To grind in valves put a light spring under the head and use a medium grade carborundum paste unless the seats are in very good condition, when fine grade paste may be used at once. Use a suction cap tool and grind with a semi-rotary movement, letting the valve rise off its seat occasionally by pressure of the spring under the head. Use paste sparingly and when both seats have a smooth matt grey finish clean away all traces of the paste from both valve and port. Reinstall the valves, assembling the oil dripper caps, springs, valve retainers and valve cap to each valve in turn. On engines prior to Serial No. 4.105.508 dripper caps were not fitted but when reassembling the valves after regrinding it is advisable to fit caps.

When reassembling the valves fit new springs if the old ones are found to be shorter than the sizes specified (see FIG 1:9). Each valve is held by two springs, an outer and an inner and the springs for inlet and exhaust valves are identical. When refitting springs the end with the closer coils (shown as 'C' in FIG 1:9), should be fitted on the cylinder head side.

The valves are made of chromium nickel steel with the valve stem hard chrome plated on its bearing length. The inlet and exhaust valve on each cylinder form a 25 deg. angle between them. Two different types of valves are fitted dependant on the date of manufacture of the engine. On all XC engines and XC5 engines up to Serial No. 5.046.809 the valves are of different dimensions to those fitted to XC5 and later engines from Serial No. 5.046.810. The two different types together with all relevant dimensions can be seen in FIG 1:10.

4 The valve seats and guides are made of a special cast iron. Oversize seats and guides are available and to remove and refit, the cylinder head should first be immersed in boiling water. Before positioning the new seats and guides slightly chamfer the cylinder head, in order to avoid damage when installing. The inner diameter of the new guides is .2mm less than the original diameter. After installation the guides must be rebored to the desired dimension.

5 The rocker gear shown in FIG 1:11 is made of two shafts resting on five supports common to both shafts. The rocker arm supports Nos. 2 and 4 are interchangeable. It is essential when reassembling the rocker shafts that the oil holes should be turned inwards. The rockers are made of forged steel with hardened tips. They are held by eight identical springs with a free length of 46 mm and are of two identical types. Type number 1 (see FIG 1:11), for 2 and 4

VALVES

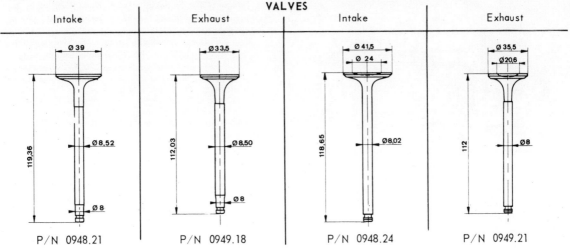

Intake	Exhaust	Intake	Exhaust
Ø 39	Ø33,5	Ø 41,5 / Ø 24	Ø 35,5 / Ø20,6
119,36 / Ø8,52 / Ø 8	112,03 / Ø8,50 / Ø 8	118,65 / Ø8,02	112 / Ø8
P/N 0948.21	P/N 0949.18	P/N 0948.24	P/N 0949.21

FIG 1:10   Valve dimensions

Inlet and 1 and 3 Exhaust and type Number 2 for 1 and 3 Inlet and 2 and 4 Exhaust.

6 The rocker pushrods are made of a special steel with cyanide treated ends. They are of two types with different lengths but the maximum permissible out of round for either is .4 mm.

The dimensions for the pushrods are as follows:
Inlet rocker pushrod, total length, 185.6 mm.
Exhaust rocker pushrod, total length, 219.5 mm.

7 Finish decarbonizing by cleaning carbon from the piston crowns. Spring an old piston ring into the bore on top of the piston and scrape with a blunt tool so that a ring of carbon is left round the periphery to prevent excessive oil consumption. Clean off thoroughly and make sure that the faces of the head and cylinder block are free from particles.

8 Refit the cylinder head as detailed in **Section 1:4**. Make sure that all pushrods are engaged with the tappets and rocker adjusting screws before tightening down.

1:6 Removing the valve timing gear and camshaft

If the cylinder head is removed ensure that the cylinder liners are set in position with the setting screws. If the cylinder head is on the engine remove the sparking plugs to allow easy rotation of the engine.

1 Remove the crankshaft pulley and its locking key, the timing gear housing and the oil rejecting ring.

2 Refer to **FIG 1:12** and remove the base screw and lockwasher from the base of the tensioner body.

3 Through the screw hole thus uncovered, insert an Allen key into the hexagonal catch of the piston, 5. Turn the key clockwise to free the sole 9 from the pressure of the spring 6.

4 Remove the tensioner attaching screws 3, and withdraw the tensioner from the cylinder block. Withdraw the oil filter from the recess in the cylinder block (see **FIG 1:13**).

5 Remove the camshaft sprocket attaching screws and take off the sprocket and timing chain.

6 Remove the screws retaining the camshaft front thrust plate and withdraw the camshaft taking care not to damage the camshaft bearings during the process.

1:7 Replacing timing gear and camshaft

1 Fit the camshaft taking care not to damage the bearings or the edges of the cams and journals. Secure with thrust plate screws. Rotate the camshaft to ensure that it revolves freely in its bearings. Check

INLET

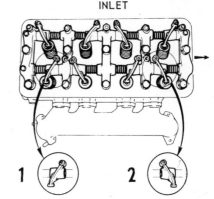

FIG 1:11   Rocker gear

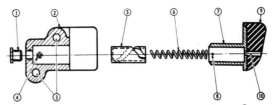

FIG 1:12   Exploded view of the timing chain tensioner

Key to Fig 1:12   1 Base screw and lockwasher
2 Tensioner body   3 Attachment holes   4 Oil intake
5 Piston   6 Spring   7 Dowel   8 Pin   9 Rubber sole
10 Chain lubrication hole

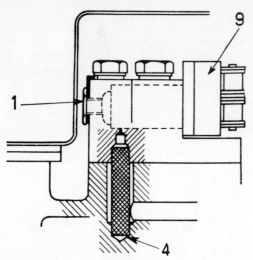

FIG 1:13 Chain tensioner oil filter in position in cylinder block

Key to Fig 1:13   1 Tensioner base screw   4 Oil filter
9 Tensioner sole head

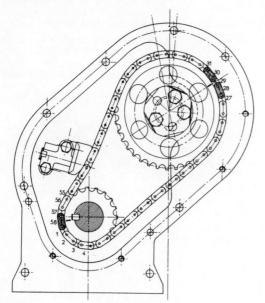

FIG 1:14   The timing gear assembled for correct valve timing

the camshaft end float at the thrust plate. This should be .003 inch to .006 inch.

2 Fit the camshaft sprocket to the camshaft temporarily and position the mark on the sprocket at approximately the two o'clock position (see **FIG 1:14**).

3 Turn the crankshaft to bring the key and timing mark to the nine o'clock position.

4 Remove the camshaft sprocket and fit to the timing chain so that the timing mark on the sprocket is positioned centrally between the two copper plated links of the chain.

5 Holding the camshaft sprocket and chain in this position, loop the chain over the crankshaft sprocket so that the timing mark on the crankshaft sprocket engages the chain at the other single copper plated link. These timing marks can all be clearly seen in **FIG 1:14**. Place the camshaft sprocket on the camshaft and install the retaining screws. Check that the timing marks and copper links are still correctly positioned, then tighten the camshaft sprocket retaining screws to a torque of 13 to 18 lb ft.

6 Check the tensioner. Make sure that the piston moves freely inside the dowel (see **FIG 1:12**), and that the filter, the oil intake holes on the chain tensioner and the chain lubricating holes on the sole are clean and clear.

7 Fit the filter into the recess in the cylinder block.

8 Fit the spring and piston into the tensioner dowel and instal in the tensioner body, compressing the assembly loosely by turning the piston clockwise with an Allen key inserted in the hole in the base of the tensioner body.

9 Place the tensioner in position on the cylinder block and attach with the locating screws and tighten the screws to a torque of 3.5 to 5.5 lb ft.

10 Release the tensioner by turning clockwise with the Allen key inserted through the hole in the base. Fit and lock the screw in the base. **Do not force or assist the tensioner sole against the chain in any way during the above operation.**

11 Fit the oil deflector ring on the crankshaft and install the timing cover, using a new gasket. Refit the crankshaft pulley and locking key and tighten the starting grip to a torque of 72 to 86 lb ft. Peen to lock.

Timing gear adjustment check:

When the valve timing is correctly set, with the crankshaft sprocket timing mark on the fifty eighth link of the chain, the camshaft sprocket timing mark will be on the twenty-ninth link of the chain. The timing chain and sprockets, however, will only take up this position once in every fifty eight revolutions of the crankshaft.

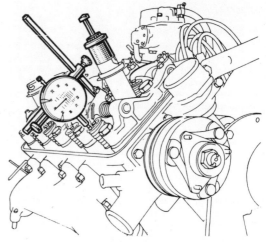

FIG 1:15   Timing adjustment check

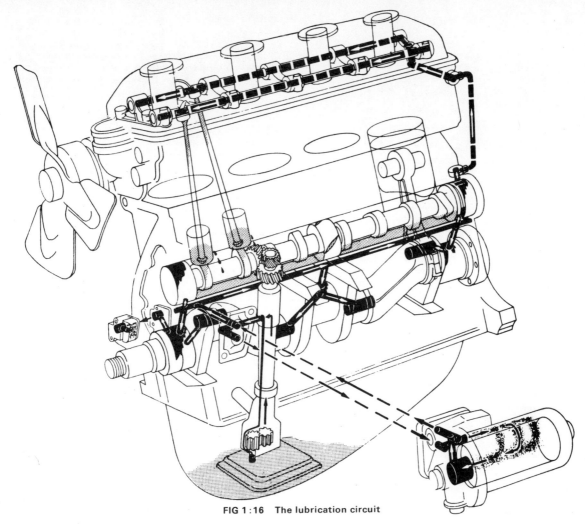

FIG 1:16   The lubrication circuit

It is possible to carry out a quick check of the timing with the aid of a measuring rod, the dimensions for which are given in the Technical Data at the end of this manual. Proceed as follows:

1 Remove the sparking plugs and the rocker cover.
2 Adjust the exhaust rocker on number 4 cylinder to .7mm clearance.
3 Place the check rod into the spark plug well of number 4 cylinder. Bring the piston to exactly TDC on the compression stroke and screw the knurled nut on the rod down to the TDC mark.
4 Fix a dial test indicator gauge onto the intermediate rocker support as shown in **FIG 1:15**. Bring the gauge finder onto the cup of the valve.
5 Slowly rotate the engine until the hand of the dial gauge just starts to move, indicating that the exhaust valve has started to open.
6 Check that the reference dash EO, on the check rod comes on a level with the knurled nut upper face. Should the reference mark fail to appear in the correct position, remove the timing gear and adjust correctly as in the preceding instructions.

7 Remove the check rod, the dial gauge and its support and readjust the exhaust rocker of number 4 cylinder to its correct clearance. Reinstall the rocker cover and the spark plugs.

The displacement between TDC and the EO mark on the check rod is 70.7mm. Owing to the slant of the spark plug well this corresponds to an actual displacement of 68.3mm for the piston.

1:8 Removing and refitting the oil pump

The pressure lubrication for the engine is provided by a classical meshing type oil pump, driven by the camshaft. The capacity of the sump is 4 litres or .88 gallon, and the recommended oil for all normal use is Esso Extra Motor Oil 20W/30-40 or Esso Oil SAE.40. For cold weather driving change to Esso Oil SAE.20. The flow of the lubricating oil through the engine and the position of the oil pump and filter can be seen in **FIG 1:16**.

To remove the oil pump first drain the sump of oil and remove the sump. Unscrew the cap nut on the side of the

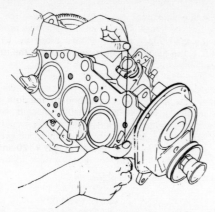

FIG 1:17 Installing the oil pump. The oil pump drive gear must be positioned so that the slot is in line with the threaded hole of No. 12 cylinder head bolt

cylinder block to uncover the pump fixing screw. Remove this screw and lift out the oil pump.

To refit the oil pump and get correct orientation of the distributor, rotate the engine to bring number 4 cylinder piston to TDC. Install the oil pump so that the distributor drive slot in the spindle points to No. 12 cylinder head stud with the large offset of the drive towards the engine (see **FIG 1:17**). Refit pump fixing screw and cap nut.

Using a new cork gasket refit the sump.

1:9 Removing the clutch and flywheel

The removal of the clutch and flywheel with the engine in the car necessitates the removal of the rear axle in order to first remove the gearbox. This operation is detailed in **Section 5:4.**

With the gearbox removed, mark the clutch plate in relation to the flywheel in order to facilitate correct reassembly. Slacken each of the six retaining bolts approximately one turn at a time, working diagonally across the clutch, until all the pressure has been removed from the diaphragm spring.

Remove the six bolts attaching the flywheel to the crankshaft and remove the flywheel. The flywheel and crankshaft bear location marks which must be lined up when reassembling.

After prolonged slipping and wear of the clutch linings, the bottom of the flywheel (see **FIG 1:18**), may be found to be scored. If this has happened, it will be necessary to true up this surface on a lathe. The same thickness of metal removed must then be removed from the face on which the clutch mechanism rests, so as not to alter the spring tension.

Two types of flywheel are in service. On earlier models the depth P is 25.9mm and on later installations the depth is 25.5mm. This of course means that there are also two types of driven disc and the discs are not interchangeable. Flywheels are interchangeable provided that the appropriate driven disc is used.

Refitting:

Ensure that the mounting face of the flywheel and the crankshaft flange are clean and free from burrs. Line up the location marks and press the flywheel into position.

Fit the retaining bolts and tighten them to a torque of 44 to 47 lb ft.

Place the clutch disc in position on the flywheel with the location marks aligned. Fit the retaining bolts and tighten to a torque of 11 to 18 lb ft, having centred the driven plate with a spare gearbox shaft or a suitable mandrel.

1:10 Splitting big-ends, removing rods and pistons

1 Remove the cylinder head as detailed in **Section 1:4.**
2 Drain the oil and remove the sump.
3 Unscrew the big-end bolts a few turns (see **FIG 1:19**), and tap them to release the connecting rods

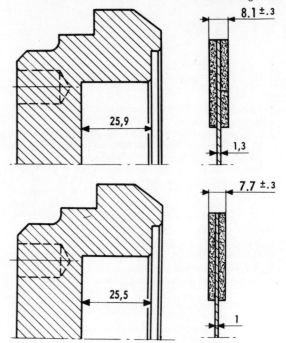

FIG 1:18 Flywheel repair dimensions

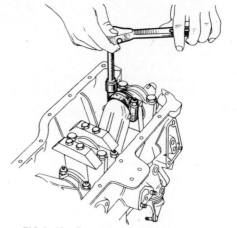

FIG 1:19 Removing the big-end cap nuts

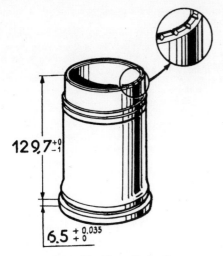

129,7 $^{+0}_{-1}$

6,5 $^{+0.035}_{+0}$

FIG 1:20   The cylinder liner

top. A rubber joint provides tightness between the liner and the cylinder block. The installed liners must protrude above the top surface of the cylinder block by .015 to .075mm. If the measurement is less than this the rubber seals at the base of the liners must be renewed.

The liners are identified at the factory by one, two, three or four notches on the lower rim. These indicate the liner diameter range and correspond to the four sizes of piston also available. When installing liners ensure that these grading marks are fitted to face the camshaft side of the engine. The cylinder liners and the grading marks referred to above can be seen in **FIG 1:20** and the four sets of dimensions are given in the table following:

Liner ref. mark	Liner bore mm
1	84.000 to 84.011
11	84.012 to 84.022
111	84.023 to 84.033
1111	84.034 to 84.044

from the caps. Then completely remove the bolts and detach the big-end caps. Push the pistons out of the cylinder bores and withdraw the assemblies. It may be necessary to carefully scrape the carbon formation away from the top of the cylinder bore to facilitate removal. Ensure that the connecting rod bearing shells and caps are kept in their correct sets after removal.

1:11 Pistons, rings and gudgeon pins and cylinder liners

The cylinder liners are detachable wet type liners made of centrifugal cast iron. They are positioned in the engine by a bore in the cylinder block at the bottom and by a shoulder in the cylinder head gasket joint face at the

Pistons:

The low expansion aluminium alloy pistons have an elliptical skirt with wide carving at the bottom. The piston skirts are not split. Different pistons are used on the later XC5 engines which raise the BHP of the engine from 72 to 76. The differences in the measurements can be seen in **FIG 1:21**.

Each piston is fitted with two compression and one oil scraper ring, the top compression ring being chrome plated.

The referencing of the pistons is made by means of one letter, A, B, C or D which correspond to the reference marks 1, 2, 3 or 4 on the cylinder liners, and this is stamped on top of the pistons. Also stamped on the top of the piston is the mark 'AV' with an arrow. When fitting pistons this arrow must point towards the front of the engine.

Earlier installation	Later installation
(Also used on 3-main bearing engines)	(76 & 96 hp engines)

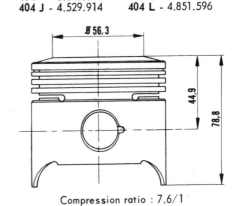

XC 5 ENGINE

404 - 5.046.809	404 C - 4.497.999	404 - 5.046.810	404 C - 4.498.001
404 J - 4.529.913	404 L - 4.851.595	404 J - 4.529.914	404 L - 4.851.596

Ø 63,2 — 43,7 — 71,6 — Compression ratio : 7.4/1

Ø 56,3 — 44,9 — 78,8 — Compression ratio : 7.6/1

FIG 1:21   Piston dimensions for XC5 and later engines

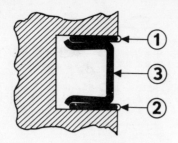

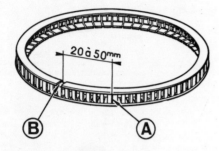

A - Expander section gap position

B - Flexible ring gap position

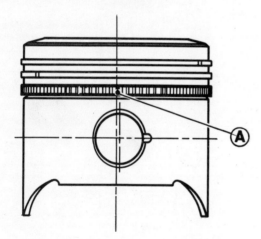

FIG 1 : 22 'Perfect Circle' oil scraper rings

Key to Fig 1 : 22   1/2 Flexible scraper sections
3 Expander centre section

The four piston sizes are as follows, the diameter being measured perpendicular to the gudgeon pin at the top and bottom of the skirt.

Ref. mark	Piston diameter in mm
A	83.940 to 83.951
B	83.951 to 83.962
C	83.963 to 83.973
D	83.973 to 83.984

Oil scraper rings, XC5 engines:

XC5 engines may have conventional oil scraper rings or 'Perfect-Circle' Scraper rings.

The 'Perfect Circle' scraper rings shown in **FIG 1 : 22** comprise three sections as follows:

1 Two flexible scraper sections 1 and 2 made of steel and chromium plated on their outside bearing face.
2 An expander section 3, also made of steel.

No reference marks are needed for installation as the parts are all symmetrical. The expander diameter is larger than the liner diameter so that the expander radially forces both flexible scraper sections outwards, resulting in uniform pressure of these sections against the liner. Because of this, the length of the expander centre section should in no case be decreased.

Installing 'Perfect Circle' scraper rings:

1 Install the expander section in the piston groove.
2 Working from the piston head, install one flexible section on top of the expander section by first engaging the flexible section end over the expander end. Move the flexible section end 20 to 50mm to the left so that end B is 20 to 50 mm left of end A (see **FIG 1 : 22**).
3 Install the other flexible section over the bottom face of the expander section in the same manner.
4 Check that the expander section ends do not overlap, then rotate the oil scraper ring assembly in the piston groove to ensure correct positioning.
5 Locate the expander section gap along the gudgeon pin axis to avoid placing this gap over one of the oil return grooves in the piston.
6 Fit the compression rings and space the gaps at 120 deg. Ensure that the brand mark near the gap is facing upwards.

When installing the pistons into the cylinder liner great care must be taken to avoid jamming the flexible sections of the scraper rings.

Connecting rods:

The treated forged steel connecting rods are fitted at the small end with a smooth bushing to provide the bearing for the gudgeon pin and at the big-end with a pair of thin removable bearing shells. An exploded view of the assembly is shown in **FIG 1 : 23**. For replacement purposes the rods are divided into six weight categories referenced 1 to 6, etched onto the big-end side with acid (see **FIG 1 : 24**). The big-end cap and big-end are marked for correct matching (see **FIG 1 : 23**).

The weights of the connecting rods, complete without bearing shells or washers are as follows:

Ref. mark	Weight in grams.
1	591 to 610
2	611 to 630
3	631 to 650
4	651 to 670
5	671 to 690
6	691 to 710

When installing the connecting rods the oiling orifice (B in **FIG 1 : 24**), should be at the side opposite to the camshaft. The connecting rod cap bolts and washers must be renewed after each dismantling.

Connecting rod bearings:

The steel and lead bearing shells are interchangeable in order to permit trueing up the crankpins. Four types of bearings are available, identified by their thickness measured at the centre of the shells.

Original thickness	1.819 to 1.825 mm
1st oversize	1.969 to 1.975 mm
2nd oversize	2.069 to 2.075 mm
3rd oversize	2.219 to 2.225 mm

Gudgeon pins:

The gudgeon pins are fitted off centre in the pistons and are held in place with circlips. The gudgeon pins and pistons are mated during manufacture and must always be kept together to prevent an overtight fit which could subsequently cause engine damage. In the case of a 'liners and pistons' exchange, remove the gudgeon pins from the new pistons which are paired with the cylinder liners. Lubricate the gudgeon pins and push them by hand into the pistons and connecting rod small-ends. Refit the circlips.

To refit the pistons and connecting rod assemblies to the engine proceed as follows:

1 If the old pistons are to be used, decarbonize the piston crowns and the ring grooves.

2 Check the piston ring gaps. Locate the piston ring in the unworn portion of the cylinder liner and check the ring gaps which should be .4 mm for both compression and oil scraper rings.

3 Assemble the piston to the connecting rod, so that when assembled in the engine, the oil squirt hole in the big-end (see **FIG 1 : 24**), is to the side opposite the camshaft and the AV marking and arrow stamped on the piston crown point to the front of the engine.

4 Fit the compression rings to the pistons with the reference marks facing upwards and the chrome faced ring in the top groove.

5 With the ring gaps spaced at 120 deg., fit the piston and connecting rods to their respective cylinder bores from which they were removed. Assemble the big-end bearing shells and caps, ensuring that the mating marks between the caps and rods are correctly related and that each assembly is in the bore from which it was removed on dismantling. Fit new big-end bolts and lockwashers and tighten the bolts to a torque of 30.7 to 34.3 lb ft.

1 : 12 Removing the crankshaft and main bearings

With the engine removed from the car (see **Section 1 : 3**), remove the transmission (see **Section 6**), the oil sump, the clutch and flywheel (see **Section 1 : 9**), and the timing chain and sprockets (see **Section 1 : 6**). Remove the sparking plugs and turn the engine upside down.

First check the crankshaft end float with a dial gauge, levering the shaft endwise. The correct clearance should be .08 to .2 mm.

Release the connecting rods and replace the caps on their respective rods. Remove the main bearing bolts and remove the bearing caps.

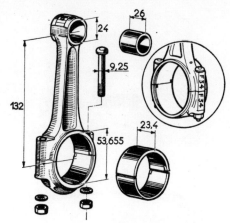

FIG 1 : 23 Connecting rod and component parts. Dimensions are in millimetres. Inset shows mating marks on the rod and big-end bearing cap

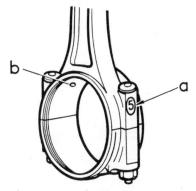

FIG 1 : 24 Connecting rod big-end

Key to Fig 1 : 24   **A** Code mark for weight identification **B** Oil hole which must be at the side opposite to the camshaft when installed

XC engines:

The front and centre main bearing caps are aligned by elastic location keys (see **FIG 1 : 25**), while the rear bearing cap is located on its studs. The centre and front main bearing caps can be identified by casting pips on the side of the cap, one pip for the front bearing cap and two pips for the centre.

XC5 and later engines:

On XC5 engines the cylinder block has been changed and a crankshaft with 5 main bearings has been installed. The bearing caps can again be identified by casting ribs on the side of the cap as seen in **FIG 1 : 26**, as follows:
Rear intermediate bearing cap No. 2: 2 ribs.
Front intermediate bearing cap No. 4: 1 rib.

The centre bearing cap 3, and the front bearing cap 5, have the same width (30 mm), and are identified by ribs on their rear faces as follows:
Centre cap No. 3:   2 ribs
Front cap No. 5:   1 rib.

Remove the crankshaft together with the end thrust washers and the bearing half shells.

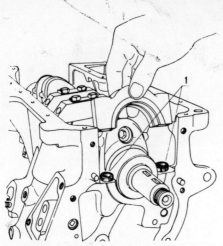

FIG 1:25 Front and centre locating dowels

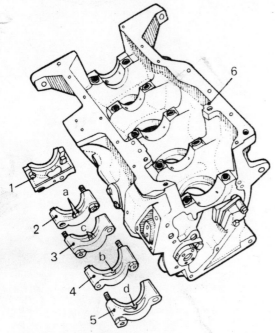

FIG 1:26 Front and centre main bearing locating dowels

Carefully clean the cylinder block and all parts removed in the dismantling. Check the condition of the journals and the crankpins. Both the main journals and the crankpins can be rectified up to a definite oversize but this is a job which must be carried out by a skilled operator with specialized equipment.

Before reinstalling the crankshaft, remove the blanking screws from the crankpin lubricating lines and flush through to ensure a full flow of oil.

Installing the crankshaft:

1 Install the main bearing half shells into the corresponding location on the cylinder block.

2 Carefully place the crankshaft onto the bearings in the cylinder block.

3 Fit the lateral thrust flanges, original size, on both sides of the rear main bearing (see **FIG 1:27**), with the bronze face towards the crankshaft.

4 Install the rear main bearing cap equipped with its half shell but without the lateral seals. Fit the centre and front cap complete with their half shells. (On XC5 engines, also fit the intermediate caps). Tighten the main bearing caps to a torque of 50 to 58 lb ft.

5 Check the longitudinal end play. Fix the dial gauge support in a suitable position (see **FIG 1:28**), and bring the dial gauge sender to rest on the end of the crankshaft.

6 Push the crankshaft fully forward and take a reading of the end float on the gauge. The end float should be between .003 to .008 inch. Should the end float exceed these figures fit oversize thrust washers which are available for service.

7 Remove the rear bearing cap and install the rubber side joints on each side of the bearing cap. Fit the special tool No. 80110Z to compress the joints, use oil to lubricate the assembly and install the assembly in position on the block (see **FIG 1:29**).

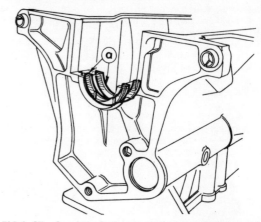

FIG 1:27 Crankshaft thrust washers at the rear main bearing

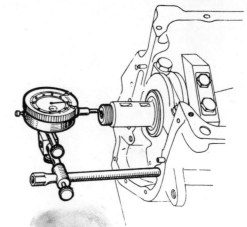

FIG 1:28 Method of checking crankshaft end float

20

8 Fit the bearing cap screws finger tight and withdraw the assembly tool. Tighten the cap screws to the specified torque of 50 to 58 lb ft.

9 Cut off the rubber side seals .020 inch above the crankcase face.

1:13 Oil filter

Clean oil for lubrication of the engine is provided by the oil filter, which is fitted in an horizontal position between the pump and the lubrication circuit (see **FIG 1:16**). The filter body is made of light alloy and is fitted with a cleanable cartridge which should be cleaned at each occasion of draining the sump. The capacity of the filter is approximately 1 pint.

On later cars an 'Easi-change', or Lockheed, disposable filter cartridge is used. This should be changed every 6000 miles (10,000 km).

The pressure switch, which is fitted onto the filter body, switches off the red tell-tale light on the facia panel as soon as the oil pressure reaches 10 lb/sq in.

1:14 Reassembling stripped engine

All dismantling and reassembling operations have been given in the various Sections, so that it is simply a matter of tackling the tasks in the correct sequence. Always fit new gaskets, which are normally available in complete sets, and lubricate all running surfaces with clean engine oil.

First fit the crankshaft, followed by the cylinder liners, if removed, and then the piston and connecting rod assemblies. Next fit the timing gear housing support, the camshaft and the timing gear.

Install the flywheel and clutch, then the oil pump, ensuring correct meshing to enable the distributor to be timed. Install the oil sump.

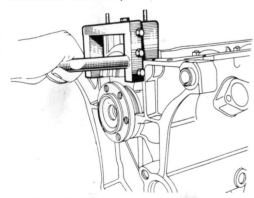

FIG 1:29   Fitting rear main bearing cap seals

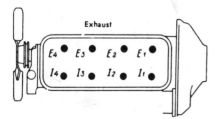

FIG 1:30   Inlet and exhaust valve numbering

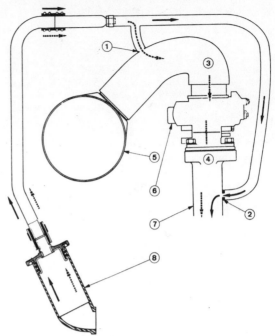

FIG 1:31   Showing the operation of the crankcase ventilation system

Key to Fig 1:31   1 Calibrated orifice   2 Opening $\frac{1}{16}$ inch   3 Air intake   4 Carburetter flange   5 Air cleaner 6 Carburetter   7 Inlet manifold   8 Separator and intake from crankcase

Next fit the valve pushrods and the cylinder head and then all the external components, i.e. Petrol pump, oil filter, carburetter, distributor, generator, starter and fan belt. Fill the engine with oil.

1:15 Replacing engine in the car

1 Sling the engine and position it diagonally in the engine compartment as for removal.

2 Align the gearbox drive shaft to engage with the splines in the clutch driven plate and slide the engine rearwards until the clutch housing is positioned on the rear of the engine. Fit the attachment screws.

3 Lower the engine onto the front mountings and fit the mounting attachment nuts.

4 Install the engine components and connections removed during engine removal, by reversing the removal procedure.

5 Refill the cooling system, check the engine oil, install and align the bonnet.

1:16 Rocker clearance adjustment

To obtain correct rocker clearances the engine must be cold when adjustment is made. Adjustment is carried out in the normal way, i.e. with a feeler gauge inserted between the valve stem and the rocker arm or tappet and screwing in or out on the adjusting screw.

The rocker clearances should be set at .004 inch for inlet and .010 inch for exhaust. To save time and many turns of the engine it will be found that the following table used in conjunction with **FIG 1:30** will be useful.

Valve fully open	Adjust clearances
E.1	I.3 E.4
E.3	I.4 E.2
E.4	I.2 E.1
E.2	I.1 E.3

After the engine has been run for approximately 100 miles, the cylinder head bolts should be checked and tightened to the correct torque and the rocker clearances readjusted to their correct figure. This must again be carried out with the engine cold.

1:17 Closed crankcase ventilation

From 1966 the system shown in **FIG 1:31** was fitted in order to prevent the escape of crankcase fumes into the atmosphere. No maintenance is required other than an occasional cleaning of the metal filter in the separator.

At idling speeds the gases follow the circuit shown with the solid arrows through the calibrated orifice 2 into the inlet manifold while at full throttle they are taken into the air intake at the calibrated orifice 1. In normal running both circuits are in use depending upon the position of the throttle butterfly.

1:18 Fault diagnosis

(a) Engine will not start

1 Defective coil
2 Faulty distributor capacitor (condenser)
3 Dirty, pitted or incorrectly set contact breaker points
4 Ignition wires loose or insulation faulty
5 Water on sparking plug leads
6 Battery discharged, corrosion on terminals
7 Faulty or jammed starter
8 Sparking plug leads wrongly connected
9 Vapour lock in fuel lines
10 Defective fuel pump
11 Overchoking or underchoking
12 Blocked petrol filter or carburetter jets
13 Leaking valves or sticking valves
14 Valve timing incorrect
15 Ignition timing incorrect

(b) Engine stalls

1 Check 1, 2, 3, 4, 5, 10, 11, 12 and 13 in (a)
2 Sparking plugs defective or gaps incorrect
3 Retarded ignition
4 Mixture too weak
5 Water in fuel system
6 Petrol tank vent blocked
7 Incorrect valve clearances

(c) Engine idles badly

1 Check 2 and 7 in (b)
2 Air leak at manifold joint
3 Slow-running control screw out of adjustment
4 Air leak in carburetter
5 Over-rich mixture
6 Worn piston rings
7 Worn valve stems or guides
8 Weak exhaust valve springs

(d) Engine misfires

1 Check 1, 2, 3, 4, 5, 8, 10, 12, 13, 14 and 15 in (a), 2, 3 4 and 7 in (b)
2 Weak or broken valve springs

(e) Engine overheats

See Chapter 4

(f) Compression low

1 Check 13 in (a), 6 and 7 in (c) and 2 in (d)
2 Worn piston ring grooves
3 Scored or worn cylinder liners

(g) Engine lacks power

1 Check 3, 10, 11, 12, 13, 14 and 15 in (a); 2, 3, 4 and 7 in (b); 6 and 7 in (c) and 2 in (d). Also check (e) and (f)
2 Leaking joint washers
3 Fouled sparking plugs
4 Automatic advance not operating

(h) Burnt valves or seats

1 Check 13 in (a); 7 in (b) and 2 in (d). Also check (e)
2 Excessive carbon around valve seats and head

(j) Sticking valves

1 Check 2 in (d)
2 Bent valve stem
3 Scored valve stem or guide
4 Incorrect valve clearance

(k) Excessive cylinder liner wear

1 Check 11 in (a)
2 Lack of oil
3 Dirty oil
4 Piston rings gummed up or broken
5 Badly fitting piston rings
6 Connecting rod bent

(l) Excessive oil consumption

1 Check 6 and 7 in (c) and check (k)
2 Ring gaps too wide
3 Oil return holes in piston choked with carbon
4 Scored cylinder liners
5 Oil level too high
6 External oil leaks
7 Ineffective valve stem oil seals

(m) Crankshaft and connecting rod bearing failure

1 Check 2 in (k)
2 Restricted oilways
3 Worn journals or crankpins
4 Loose bearing caps
5 Extremely low oil pressure
6 Bent connecting rods

(n) Internal water leaks (see Chapter 4)

(o) Poor water circulation (see Chapter 4)

(p) Corrosion (see Chapter 4)

(q) High fuel consumption (see Chapter 2)

(r) Engine vibration

1 Loose generator bolts
2 Mounting rubbers loose or ineffective
3 Exhaust pipe mountings too tight
4 Misfiring due to mixture, ignition or mechanical faults

CHAPTER 2

THE FUEL SYSTEM

2:1 Fuel pump, operating principles

All the XC series engines use a mechanically operated diaphragm type fuel pump which may be manufactured by either AC, Guiot or SEV. They are all very similar in construction and operation, and the instructions given in this Section for the AC may be easily adapted to suit the other two makes. An exploded view of the fuel pump is shown in **FIG 2:1.**

The rocker arm, actuated by the camshaft, moves the diaphragm up and down. When the diaphragm is down, fuel is drawn into the pump via the inlet valve. On the upward movement of the diaphragm the inlet valve is closed, the outlet valve opens and fuel is pumped through the outlet pipe to the carburetter.

2:2 Routine maintenance

To clean the filter screen, detach the main fuel pipe hose from the pump and plug the hose to prevent fuel loss. Remove the bowl and lift off the screen. Wash the screen and bowl in paraffin and blow through the screen with compressed air. Clean out the pump chamber if necessary, and renew the bowl gasket.

Refit the screen and bowl and tighten the holding screw firmly by hand. Check that the pipe hose is fully engaged with the pump pipe.

2:3 Removing and dismantling the fuel pump

Detach the main fuel pipe hose from the pump and plug the hose to prevent fuel loss. Disconnect the carburetter feed pipe from the pump. Remove the attaching nuts and remove the fuel pump and gasket.

Remove the bowl, gasket and filter screen as detailed in **Section 2:2.** Mark across the flanges of the pump cover and body to ensure correct relationship when reassembling. Remove the pump cover.

Release the diaphragm assembly by depressing and turning it through 90 deg. Carefully prise out the valves and remove the gaskets. Do not remove the rocker arm unless excessive wear of the arm and associated components is evident.

Inspect the rocker arm and components for wear. To renew, remove the rocker arm pin retainers, tap out the pin and remove the component parts. Install the new rocker arm, the link with a spacing washer on each side, and the arm spring. Fit the pin and secure it with new retainers.

To renew the diaphragm rod oil seal, scrape away the staked metal securing the seal retainer and the body boss. Withdraw the retainer and the seal. Install two new oil seal washers and a new retainer if the original was damaged during removal. Stake the body boss at four points to secure the retainer.

FIG 2:1 Fuel pump—exploded

2:4 Reassembling the fuel pump

Install the diaphragm assembly, depressing and rotating it through 90 deg. to engage the link and also to align the diaphragm tab with the lug of the body.

Clean the valve recesses of the body, and if necessary remove any burrs left by the staking indentations so that new valves can be correctly seated in the body.

Install new gaskets and valves.

Assemble the filter screen, gasket and bowl.

Assemble the pump cover as follows:

1 Push the rocker arm towards the pump until the diaphragm is level with the body face flange.

2 Place the pump upper cover in position so that the marks made across the flanges during disassembly are aligned.

3 Fit the cover attaching screws and tighten until the heads just engage the lockwashers.

4 Operate the rocker arm several times to align the diaphragm. Then, with the rocker arm held away from the pump so as to hold the diaphragm at the top of its stroke, tighten the cover screws diagonally and evenly.

2:5 Testing the fuel pump

The fuel pump can be tested for both capacity and pressure. The pressure test is made to check for excessively high or low pressures. Low pressure indicates that the pump stroke is relatively short, an indication of worn linkage. High pressure can be caused only by installing the wrong pump or the wrong pump pressure spring during rebuilding. High pressure causes the carburetter float chamber level to rise, which enriches the mixture. In some cases, high pressure forces the needle valve off its seat and causes the carburetter to flood.

Pressure test:

To make a pressure test, disconnect the line leading into the carburetter. Use a proper fitting and 'T' adaptor as shown in **FIG 2:2** to connect a gauge into the line.

Start the engine and let it run at slow-running. A good average pressure is from 3 to 5 lb/sq in.

Capacity test:

The capacity test determines the ability of the pump to produce a specified quantity of fuel in a given time. To make this test, disconnect the rubber hose from the tester and insert it in a pint container. Start the engine and measure the time required to pump 1 pint of fuel. Most pumps will deliver 1 pint in 1 minute.

Road test:

A quick road test of the efficiency of the fuel system is to run the car at high speed while keeping the gear-lever in second gear. A good fuel pump will permit the car to attain speeds up to 50 mile/hr in second gear. A defective fuel pump will permit the car to attain a high speed but it will then slow down rapidly.

The test results should not be confused with similar results obtained with a defective ignition system which will allow the car to attain a critical speed, and will maintain it regardless of additional throttle opening. A defective fuel pump will cause the car to slow down rapidly after the carburetter runs out of fuel.

To check the pump after removal from the engine, work the rocker arm by hand. When a finger is placed over the inlet port, the pump should develop an appreciable suction after a few strokes, and maintain a vacuum for a few seconds. The pump should also hold pressure for a few seconds against a finger held over the outlet port when the rocker arm has been pressed towards the pump and then released.

2:6 Carburetter, Solex PBICA
Operating principles:

Solex carburetters are quite conventional in design, having the usual six circuits: float, idle, second idle stage, main jet for high speeds, acceleration and power circuits. Some of the carburetters have a starting circuit in place of a choke to assist in enriching the mixture for ease in starting a cold engine.

Dust-proofing is obtained by special construction of the carburetter, so that the air required for ventilating the float chamber, for the slow-running mixture, and for the emulsification of the main spraying mixture as well as the air for the starting device, is all passed through the filter normally fitted to the carburetter.

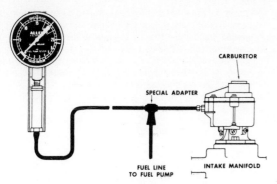

FIG 2:2 Fuel pump pressure test

It must be borne in mind that the restriction imposed by a clogged air cleaner will reduce the volume of air, and consequently mixture which the engine can inspire, and so lead to power loss. When this happens, miles to the gallon will fall.

The Solex bi-starter is a small auxiliary carburetter integral with the main carburetter to ensure easy starting from cold, and to help 'get-away' until the engine is warm enough to function satisfactorily without its aid. It has two adjustable units to provide a correct balance of air and petrol.

1 The air jet (Ga) meters the air supply (see **FIGS 2:3** and **2:5**).
2 The petrol jet (2) regulates the petrol.

To start the engine when cold:

1 Fully pull out the dashboard control to which the bi-starter lever is connected. In this position, it gives a very rich mixture which is essential for cold running.
2 Almost immediately after starting, the engine begins to warm up; the dashboard control should be pushed into the bi-starter position, that is, about halfway, when a marked resistance will be felt, indicating that the correct position has been reached.

3 At this stage the mixture strength is considerably reduced, for the volume of air inspired by the engine increases proportionately to the rise in engine speed as it continues to warm up, while the petrol supply is restricted. The strength of the mixture is sufficient to ensure immediate get-away without stalling as the accelerator is depressed.
4 As soon as the engine is warm enough (usually after driving a few hundred yards), to dispense with the bi-starter, the dashboard control must be pushed fully home, thus putting the starting device completely out of action.

When idling the mixture strength is provided by the idling or pilot jet (gn), the air bleed (u), the volume control screw (w), the last decreasing the mixture strength when turned in a clockwise direction, and vice versa. For normal running, driving at cruising speeds, the fuel is provided by the main jet (Gg), and the main air supply by the choke tube (K). The correct balance of mixture is further automatically maintained by the additional air supply in the form of a calibrated jet called the air correction jet (a). Letters in brackets refer to **FIG 2:3**.

The accelerator pump:

When the throttle is closed, the expansion spring in the pump chamber forces the diaphragm (M), into a definite position, allowing the chamber on the left to fill with petrol.

The diaphragm is connected to the accelerator by an adjustable linkage fixed to the throttle spindle; thus, the instant the throttle is opened, the spindle turns and the link operating with it forces the diaphragm to the left, ejecting the petrol in the pump chamber through the pump jet (4) and via the ejector (2) projecting into the choke tube area (see **FIG 2:4**).

The volume of the injection is regulated by the adjustment of the linkage. The size of the jet (4) controls the speed of the injection.

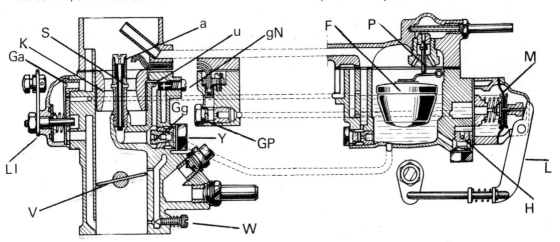

FIG 2:3 Carburetter, diagrammatic

Key to Fig 2:3 **a** Correction jet **F** Float **Ga** Starter air jet **Gg** Main jet **Gp** Pump jet **Gs** Starter petrol jet
gN Pilot jet **H** Pump valve **K** Choke tube **L** Pump lever **L1** Starter lever **M** Pump diaphragm **P** Needle valve
s Emulsion tube **u** Idling air bleed **V** Throttle butterfly **W** Volume control screw **Y** Main jet carrier

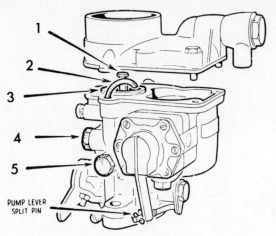

FIG 2:4   Normal running jets

Key to Fig 2:4   1 Air correction jet   2 Pump nozzle
3 Choke tube   4 Pump jet   5 Main jet

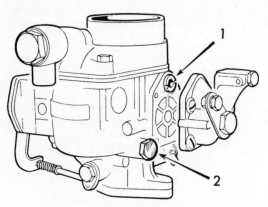

FIG 2:5   Cold start jets

Key to Fig 2:5   1 Starter air jet   2 Starter fuel jet

Starting checks:

With a cold engine, do not forget to push in fully the dashboard control as soon as the engine is warm enough to run satisfactorily on the main carburetter output.

On warm days, if the engine is not stone cold, it is usually possible to start it with the dashboard control pulled out only to the halfway position.

If an instant start is not made, check possible causes as follows:

Remove and clean the starter petrol jet 2 (see **FIG 2:5**). Blow through it with compressed air or a cycle pump. If the engine has not been run for some time, prime the petrol pump, clean and reset the sparking plugs.

The battery may be low and need recharging. A point often overlooked is that while strong enough to operate the electric starter the current may, in consequence, be completely absorbed, leaving none to give a spark at the plug points.

If the engine is hot and it does not start immediately, depress the accelerator, operate the starter, and the engine should start within a few seconds. With a hot engine and the ignition and carburetter correctly adjusted, it is normally possible to start the engine on the pilot jet output—that is, with the throttle closed.

2:7 Slow-running adjustment

1 This adjustment is of considerable importance and depends on the mechanical perfection of both the engine and carburetter. Compressions must be equal, the ignition system in good condition, and the induction system free from air leaks. The throttle pull-off spring must pull the throttle back to its stop (closed) position. All nuts and screws used in the assembly of the carburetter must be tight.

2 Check that the volume control screw has not been broken or distorted by overtightening. If it has a new screw must be fitted.

3 Adjust the slow-running as follows:
Start and run the engine until it attains its normal operating temperature. Set the throttle adjusting screw until the idling speed is on the high side.

4 Slacken the volume control screw until the engine begins to hunt, then screw it in gradually until the hunting disappears.

5 If the engine speed is too high, reset the throttle control screw to slow it down to an idling speed of about 500 rev/min. This may cause a resumption of slight hunting. If it does, turn the volume control screw gently in a clockwise direction until the idling is correct.

Routine maintenance:

The carburetter must be kept in good condition. To clean it remove the jets and blow through them with compressed air. At the same time blow through the carburetter channels.

All the jets are fitted externally and are easily accessible as follows:

1 The main jet (Gg) is screwed into the submerged end of its carrier or holder (5) (see **FIG 2:4**).

2 The emulsion tube (S) is held in position by the correction jet (a). Access is obtained by removing the air cleaner (see **FIG 2:3**).

3 The position of the starter air jet and the starter petrol jet can be seen in **FIG 2:5**.

4 The needle valve and float can be removed by unscrewing the slot headed screws which secure the float chamber cover, and lifting off the cover.

Make sure that all assembly screws are tight and check that there is no side play in the throttle spindle. If the acceleration is poor, make sure that the jet (Gp) is not choked although this would normally affect the general performance. Never interfere with the diaphragm in the accelerator pump. If it needs replacing, replace the whole assembly, which is fixed to the carburetter by the four corner screws.

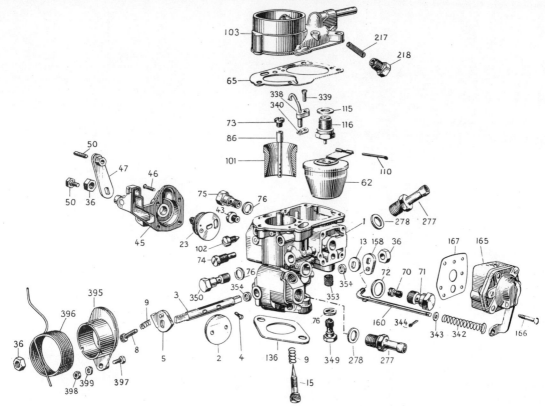

FIG 2:6   Exploded view of the Solex PBICA carburetter

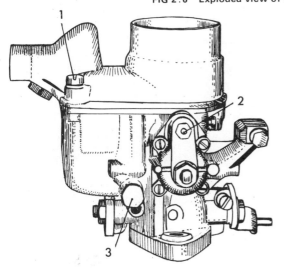

FIG 2:7   View of carburetter showing starter valve assembly

2:8 Dismantling the carburetter

An exploded view of the carburetter is shown in **FIG 2:6** and the dismantling procedure is as follows:

1 Refer to **FIG 2:7** and remove the three float chamber cover screws 1, and lift off the cover. Remove the four screws and lift off the starter valve assembly 2. This is the enrichment valve for cold starting. Remove the starter fuel jet 3.

2 Refer to **FIG 2:8** and remove the air correction jet 2, and the emulsion tube under it. Remove the pump discharge jet 1.

3 From the inside of the float chamber remove the float lever and pin 3, and the float assembly 4.

4 Take out the four screws holding the accelerating pump diaphragm and spring assembly 5, and disconnect the pump from the operating link and connecting rod 7.

5 Remove the main metering jet and holder assembly 6.

6 Remove the idle mixture adjusting screw 8, and the pump check valve from underneath the float bowl.

7 Remove the accelerating pump jet 9, and the pilot jet 10.

8 Remove the idle air bleed 11.

Inspecting and cleaning:

Clean all parts in carburetter cleaner, follow with a solvent bath and blow dry. The diaphragms should be cleaned only in solvent, never in carburetter cleaner. Blow compressed air through all passageways and jets to ensure that they are not obstructed.

Check the throttle shaft for wear. If it appears to be excessively loose, renew the shaft.

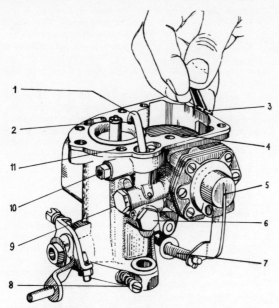

FIG 2:8 View with float chamber cover removed

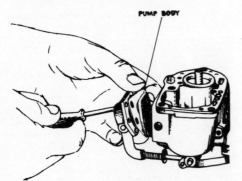

FIG 2:9 Fitting the pump body centralizing screws

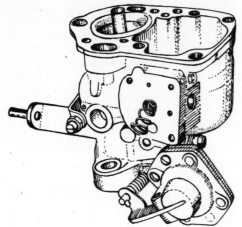

FIG 2:10 Assembling the pump diaphragm spring

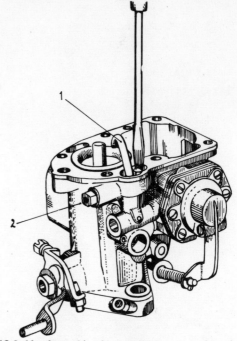

FIG 2:11 Assembly of pump discharge nozzle and pilot jet

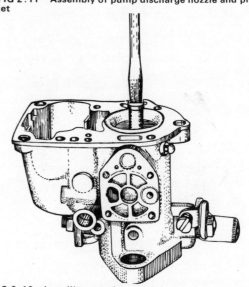

FIG 2:12 Installing emulsion tube and air correction jet

FIG 2:13 Installing the pump check valve

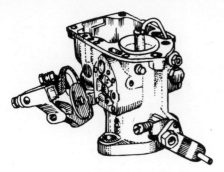

FIG 2:14 Replacing the starter unit

Shake the float to check for leaks and renew it if it contains liquid. Check the float arm needle contacting surfaces and renew the float assembly if it is grooved.

Always replace the accelerator pump diaphragm as it deteriorates on exposure to air. Test the pump check valve by sucking on it. It should pass air one way but seal the other way.

A carburetter kit is available for carburetter overhaul. It contains new parts to replace those which wear the most, plus a complete set of gaskets. Each kit contains a matched fuel inlet needle and seat assembly, which should be replaced each time the carburetter is taken apart, otherwise there is a serious risk of leaks.

2:9 Reassembling the carburetter

1 Install the washer, spring and pump cover assembly over the pump control rod and secure with a cotter pin.
2 Position the diaphragm assembly over the pump body and then insert and tighten the two centralized cover-to-body screws (see **FIG 2:9**).
3 Position a new pump body gasket and the pump diaphragm spring (see **FIG 2:10**), and then install and tighten the four retaining screws.
4 Install the pilot jet (idle jet) and the pump discharge nozzle (see **FIG 2:11**).
5 Install the idle air bleed.
6 Install the main metering jet and holder assembly.
7 Install the pump jet.
8 Push the emulsion tube into position and then screw in the air correction jet (see **FIG 2:12**).
9 Insert the starter air jet and the starter fuel jet.
10 Install the pump check valve and strainer assembly, and the idle mixture adjusting screw (see **FIG 2:13**). Turn the screw in until it lightly touches its seat, and then back it out two turns for a preliminary adjustment.
11 Replace the starter unit (see **FIG 2:14**). No gasket is needed. Move the control lever back and forth to make sure that it is free. The starter unit takes the place of a choke by admitting more fuel when the control lever is pulled back to the start position.
12 Install a new needle valve and seat. The fuel lever is adjusted by installing additional fibre washers under the needle valve seat. Replace the fuel filter.
13 Drop the float assembly into the fuel chamber, position a new gasket on top of the carburetter body, and then replace the float chamber cover. Install and tighten the three retaining screws.

2:10 Carburetter, Zenith 34 WIM

This type of carburetter will be found on some engines in place of the Solex which it very much resembles as will be seen from the exploded view in **FIG 2:15** and the sectional diagram of **FIG 2:16**.

Starting:

In order to obtain the rich mixture required when starting from cold, the eccentrically mounted plate 11 is closed by pulling out the choke knob on the instrument panel. At the same time the forked lever 10 rotates and, by means of the adjustable rod 26, opens the throttle

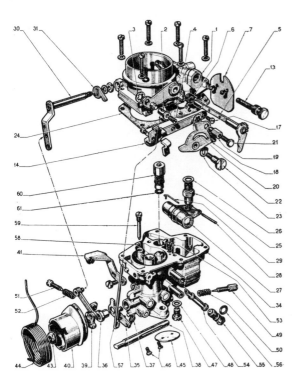

FIG 2:15 Components of Zenith carburetter 34 WIM

Key to Fig 2:15   1 Top cover   2 Clamp for 57
3 Lockwasher   4 Grub screw   5 Choke plate pivot
6 Spring   7 Choke plate   13 Filter   14 Clamp   18 Cam
and lever   19 Cable attachment   20 Lockwasher
21 Clamp screw   22 Pivot screw   23 Rubber ring
24 Gasket   25 Valve housing   26 Washer   27 Float
28 Float pivot pin   29 Link pin   30 Pump operating shaft
31 Pump operating lever   34 Carburetter body   35 Fast
idle lever   36 Bush   37 Spring   38 Butterfly spindle
39 Pump operating lever   40 Spring housing   41 Throttle
control bracket   43 Fixing screw   44 Butterfly return spring
45 Throttle butterfly   47 Pump valve   48 Washer
49 Slow-running screw   50 Spring   51 Throttle stop screw
52 Spring   53 Idle jet   54 Atomizer   55 Main jet
56 Washer   57 Fast idle rod   58 Ball   59 Ball retaining
plug   60 Pump piston   61 Washer

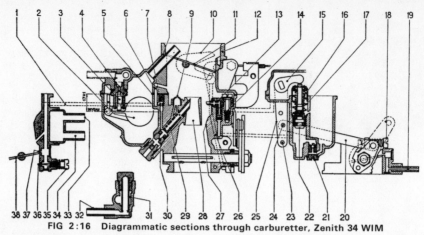

FIG 2:16 Diagrammatic sections through carburetter, Zenith 34 WIM

Key to Fig 2:16 1 Passage 2 Float 3 Needle 4 Valve 5 Float chamber 6 Calibrated air passage 7 Idle jet 8 Air correction jet 10 Forked lever 11 Choke plate 12 Top cover 13 Pump jet 14 Valve 15 Lever 16 Spring 17 Spring 18 Throttle stop screw 20 Lever arm 21 Valve 22 Piston 23-24 Pivot holes 25 Lever 26 Adjustable rod 27 Venturi 28 Venturi 29 Atomizer 30 Main jet 31 Filter 32 Inlet 35 Idle mixture screw 36 Orifice 37 Orifice 38 Butterfly

butterfly so as to produce the correct volume of mixture for a fast idle, a rapid warm-up or immediate use of the vehicle. The choke control should be progressively returned to its normal position as the engine reaches its operating temperature.

Should the driver forget to return the control knob as mentioned, provision is made for the choke plate to tilt on its pivot under the influence of the manifold depression and so open a passage for sufficient air to prevent stalling the engine by over-choking.

Slow-running adjustment:

Run the engine until it has reached its normal working temperature, then adjust the screw 18 to open the throttle butterfly to a position which gives a speed of about 670 rev/min.

Turn the mixture control screw 35 to give the highest possible engine speed then, by further operation of the screw 18, bring the engine speed back to 670 rev/min.

Screw in the screw 35 to the point where the engine starts to run roughly or stall then turn it back just sufficiently to obtain a speed of 650 rev/min.

If the correct setting is difficult to obtain, check that there are no air leaks to upset the mixture.

Fast idle adjustment:

The correct opening of the throttle butterfly when the choke control is operated is most important in securing a good start and good running while the engine is still cold.

A convenient way of obtaining this setting is as follows:

With a hot engine, close the choke sufficiently to actuate the throttle, and then adjust the length of the rod 26 to give a road speed on the level in top gear of approximately 16 mile/hr without touching the accelerator pedal.

2:11 Fault diagnosis
(a) Leakage or insufficient fuel delivered

1 Air vent in tank restricted
2 Petrol pipes blocked
3 Air leaks at pipe connections
4 Pump or carburetter filters blocked
5 Pump gaskets faulty
6 Pump diaphragm defective
7 Pump valves sticking or seating badly
8 Fuel vapourising in pipelines due to heat

(b) Excessive fuel consumption

1 Carburetter needs adjusting
2 Fuel leakage
3 Sticking controls
4 Dirty air cleaner
5 Excessive engine temperature
6 Brakes binding
7 Tyres under-inflated
8 Idling speed too high
9 Car overloaded

(c) Idling speed too high

1 Rich fuel mixture
2 Carburetter controls sticking
3 Slow-running screw incorrectly adjusted
4 Worn carburetter butterfly valve

(d) Noisy fuel pump

1 Loose mountings
2 Air leaks on suction side and at diaphragm
3 Obstruction in fuel pipe
4 Clogged pump filter

(e) No fuel delivery

1 Float needle stuck
2 Vent in tank blocked
3 Pipeline obstructed
4 Pump diaphragm stiff or damaged
5 Inlet valve in pump stuck open
6 Bad air leak on suction side of pump

CHAPTER 3

THE IGNITION SYSTEM

3:1 Description
3:2 Routine maintenance
3:3 Ignition faults
3:4 Timing the ignition

3:5 Spark plugs
3:6 Testing the ignition system
3:7 Fault diagnosis

3:1 Description

All cars covered by this manual use Ducellier or SEV distributors, which incorporate a centrifugal advance and a vacuum advance mechanism.

The vacuum unit, containing a spring-loaded diaphragm is linked to the contact breaker moving plate, and the vacuum side of the unit is connected by a pipe to the carburetter. Under part throttle conditions, the depression in the manifold actuates the contact breaker plate to advance the ignition timing.' During acceleration, when the engine is under load, the depression is not sufficient to actuate the contact breaker plate against the tension of the diaphragm, so that the plate is held in the retarded position.

The centrifugal advance mechanism consists of a cam actuated by two spring-loaded weights. As the speed of the engine increases, the weights swing outwards against the pull of the springs. This moves the cam in an anti-clockwise direction, causing the contact breaker points to open earlier and advance the timing. The distributor can be seen in **FIG 3:1.**

The coil and the condenser (capacitor) are also made by Ducellier or SEV.

For sparking plugs see **Section 3:5.**

3:2 Routine maintenance

Refer to **FIG 3:2** and remove the distributor cap. Pull the rotor squarely off the end of the mainshaft and cam. Apply a few drops of engine oil to the felt pad in the end of the cam under the rotor. Take great care to avoid oil coming into contact with the contact breaker plate or the points.

Lightly smear the cam with petroleum jelly.

Adjusting the contact breaker points:

Refer to **FIG 3:3,** and with the distributor cap and rotor removed, slacken the locking screw V.

Move the eccentric E, in the appropriate direction to obtain the correct gap through the displacement of the support S, which pivots about the axis pin A. Set the gap to .5 mm (.02 inch).

Retighten the screw V, and recheck the gap. The gap must be set and measured when the cam peak is centralized on the contact arm.

If the contact breaker points are dirty or pitted they must be cleaned by polishing them with a fine carborundum stone, taking care to keep the faces flat and square. Afterwards, wipe away all traces of dust with a non-fluffy cloth moistened in fuel.

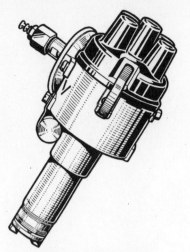

FIG 3:1   The distributor

If the contacts are very badly worn or pitted they should be renewed.

3:3 Ignition faults

If the engine runs unevenly, set it to idle at a fast speed. Taking care not to touch any metal part of the sparking plug leads, pull up the insulator sleeves and short each plug in turn, using a screwdriver with an insulated handle. Connect the screwdriver between the plug top and the cylinder head. Shorting a plug which is firing correctly will make the uneven running more pronounced. Shorting a plug in a cylinder which is not firing will make no difference.

Having located the faulty cylinder, stop the engine and remove the plug lead. Start the engine and hold the lead carefully to avoid shocks, so that the metal end is about $\frac{3}{16}$ inch away from the cylinder head. A strong regular spark shows that the fault probably lies with the plug. Remove and clean the plug or, alternatively, substitute a new plug.

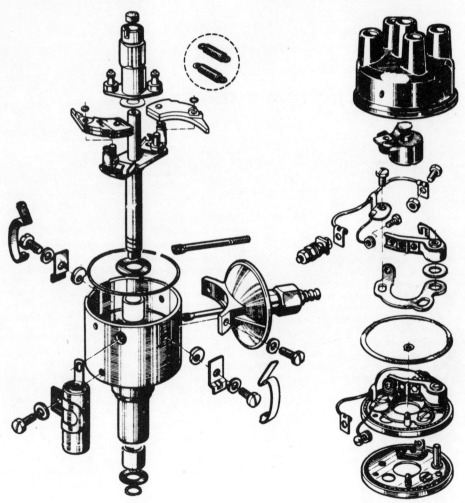

FIG 3:2   Exploded view of the distributor

If the spark is weak and irregular, check that the lead is not perished or cracked. If it appears to be defective, renew it and try another test. If there is no improvement, remove the distributot cap and wipe the inside clean and dry. Examine the carbon button for wear and the segments for burning.

Inspect the caps for cracks and tracking burns. Tracking will be indicated by a thin black line between the segments.

3:4 Timing the ignition

1 With the engine on compression stroke for No. 1 cylinder, insert a 8 mm diameter bar in the timing hole on the top righthand side of the clutch housing (see **FIG 3:4**).

2 Holding light inward pressure on the end of the bar, rotate the crankshaft until the bar drops into the timing recess in the flywheel. This is the firing point for No. 1 cylinder.

3 Fit the distributor, correctly adjusted, into the distributor support in its approximate position, and pressing down on the distributor body, turn the rotor to engage the driving slot in the drive spindle. The vacuum intake to the distributor should lie between the petrol pump outlet and the carburetter. Connect the vacuum advance pipe and the low-tension terminal to the coil.

4 Connect a timing light between the low-tension terminal on the distributor and earth. Switch on the ignition.

5 Rotate the distributor in an anticlockwise direction until the light goes out, then turn the distributor in the opposite direction until the light just lights. Tighten the support collar bolt. Check that the distributor rotor is pointing to the position of No. 1 sparking plug terminal in the distributor cap when the cap is in position. The ignition setting can be altered slightly on road test by turning the knurled adjusting nut.

3:5 Sparking plugs

Up to the end of the series with 3 main bearing engines the spark plugs are of the short base type and should be set with a spark plug gap of .6 mm (.024 inch). Plugs suitable for this engine are Marchal 36.P or AC.44.F.

On later installations, with 5 main bearing engines, the sparking plugs are of the long base type. The spark plug gap is the same. Suitable plugs are Marchal 36.HS or AC.P.44.XL.

The long base and short base plugs are not interchangeable and the engine may be extensively damaged if the incorrect type is fitted.

Inspect, clean and adjust the sparking plugs regularly. The inspection of the electrodes is particularly useful because the type and colour of the deposit gives a clue to conditions inside the combustion chamber, and is therefore helpful when tuning.

Remove the sparking plugs by loosening them a couple of turns and then blowing away loose dirt from the plug recesses with compressed air or a tyre pump. Store them in the order of removal.

Examine the plug gaskets. If they are about half their original thickness they may be used again.

Examine the firing end of the plugs to note the type of deposit. Normally, it should be powdery, and range

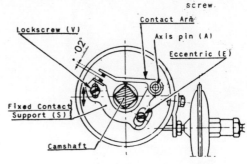

FIG 3:3 Contact breaker gap adjustment. The contact breaker gap for the Peugeot 404 is .5 mm (.02 inch)

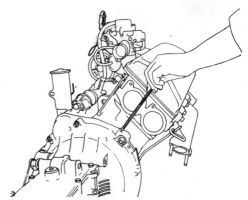

FIG 3:4 Method of finding the crankshaft position for correct ignition timing

from brown to greyish tan in colour. There will also be slight wear of the electrodes, and the general effect is one which comes from mixed periods of high-speed and low-speed driving. Cleaning and resetting the gap is all that will be required.

If the deposits are white or yellowish, they indicate long periods of constant speed driving or much low-speed city driving. Again the treatment is straightforward.

Black, wet deposits are caused by oil entering the combustion chamber past worn pistons, piston rings or down valve stems. Sparking plugs of a type which run hotter may help to alleviate the problem, but the cure is an engine overhaul.

Dry, black, fluffy deposits are usually the result of running with a rich mixture. Incomplete combustion may also be a cause and this might be traced to defective ignition or excessive idling.

Overheated sparking plugs have a white, blistered look about the centre electrode and the side electrode may be badly eroded. This may be caused by poor cooling, incorrect ignition timing, or sustained high speeds with a heavy load.

Have the sparking plugs cleaned on an abrasive blasting machine, and tested under pressure, after attention to the electrodes. File these until they are clean, bright, and parallel. When setting the electrode gap do not try to bend the centre electrode.

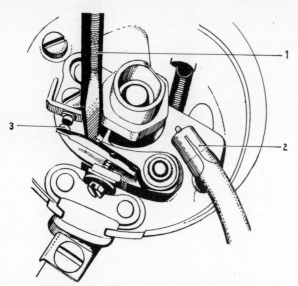

FIG 3:5 Method of testing the primary circuit

Key to Fig 3:5   1 Screwdriver   2 H.T. cable
3 Contact points

Before replacing the plugs, clean the threads with a wire brush, but do not use this brush on the electrodes. If it is found that the plugs cannot be screwed in by hand, run a tap down the threads in the cylinder head. Failing a tap, use an old sparking plug with crosscuts down the threads.

Finally tighten with a box spanner through half a turn.

3:6 Testing the ignition system

Primary circuit:

To test the primary circuit, loosen the distributor cap clips and move the cap to one side. Remove the rotor.

Turn the engine over until the contact points close and switch on the ignition.

Remove the high-tension wire leading to the centre of the distributor cap. This is the main wire from the ignition coil which supplies the high voltage to the distributor.

Hold this wire about $\frac{1}{2}$ inch from any metallic part of the engine. Open and close the contact points with a screwdriver, holding the screwdriver only against the moveable contact point as shown in **FIG 3:5**.

A good, regular spark from the high-tension wire to earth means a good primary circuit and good ignition coil.

A weak spark, or no spark at all indicates trouble with either the primary circuit or igniton coil.

Contact points:

To test the condition of the ignition contact set, turn the engine over until the contact points are open.

Refer to **FIG 3:6** and slide the screwdriver up and down making contact between the moveable point and the bottom plate of the distributor. You are now using the blade of the screwdriver and the bottom plate of the distributor as a set of contact points. A good spark from the high-tension wire to earth, after having no spark in

the previous test for the primary circuit, means that the contact points are defective.

Condenser (Capacitor):

A shorted condenser can be checked by noting, in the test for contact points, described previous to this test, whether or not the tip of the screwdriver blade sparked against the ground plate as it was slid up and down. No spark indicates either a shorted condenser or a break in the primary circuit.

This can be checked further by disconnecting the condenser case where it is attached to the distributor. Do not disconnect the condenser electrical wire.

Hold the condenser so that its case does not come into contact with any metallic part of the distributor. Repeat the test of moving the screwdriver blade up and down while holding it against the moveable point.

Ensure that the contact points are open during this test. A spark at the screwdriver tip now, which was not present with the condenser in the circuit, indicates that the condenser is shorted out.

No spark at the screwdriver tip with the condenser out of the circuit indicates that there is an open circuit somewhere in the primary circuit.

Check the small lead from the primary terminal to the moveable contact point, as this lead sometimes parts under constant flexing during operation.

Secondary circuit:

The secondary circuit cannot be tested until the primary circuit is functioning correctly.

To test the secondary circuit, turn the engine over until the contact points close. Turn on the ignition.

Hold the main high-tension wire (from the centre of the distributor cap) about $\frac{1}{2}$ inch from any metallic part of the engine. Open and close the contact points with a

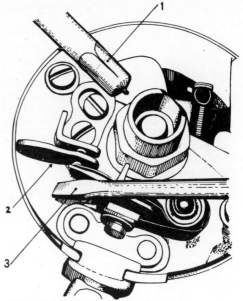

FIG 3:6 Method of testing the contact points

Key to Fig 3:6   1 H.T. cable   2 Insulator   3 Screwdriver

screwdriver blade held against the moveable point. No spark, or a weak one, from the high-tension wire to the engine indicates a defective coil or a defective main high-tension wire from the coil to the distributor. This may possibly be shorting where it runs through a metal conduit.

A good spark here, with no spark to the spark plugs, indicates that the fault lies in the distributor cap, the rotor or the spark plugs.

To check the high-tension wire from the coil to the distributor, renew it, and repeat the test.

Distributor rotor:

Test the rotor by replacing it on the distributor shaft and holding the main high-tension wire from the coil about $\frac{1}{4}$ inch from the top of the rotor. With the ignition switched on, crank the engine with the starter motor. If the high-tension spark jumps to the rotor, it is defective. If not, the cap must be defective and it should be inspected for carbon tracks which indicate the passing of high voltage current.

3:7 Fault diagnosis

(a) Engine will not fire

1 Battery discharged
2 Distributor points dirty, pitted or out of adjustment
3 Distributor cap dirty, cracked or 'tracking'
4 Carbon brush inside the distributor cap not in contact with the rotor.
5 Faulty cable or loose connection in low-tension circuit
6 Distributor rotor arm cracked
7 Faulty coil
8 Broken contact breaker spring
9 Contact points stuck open

(b) Engine misfires

1 Check 2, 3, 5 and 7 in (a)
2 Weak contact spring
3 High-tension plug and coil leads cracked or perished
4 Sparking plugs loose
5 Sparking plug insulation cracked
6 Sparking plug gap incorrect
7 Ignition timing too far advanced

NOTES

CHAPTER 4

THE COOLING SYSTEM

4:1 Description

The cooling system incorporates a radiator, a centrifugal pump, a thermoswitch and a magnetic type fan to keep the engine at its most efficient temperature. On later models the system is pressurized to 4 lb/sq inch by the fitting of a pressure/vacuum cap which allows a water temperature of 107°C (225°F) before boiling.

In the magnetic clutch fan (see **FIG 4 : 1**), the electro magnet A, is integral with the water pump pulley. The fan is loose on the water pump shaft and is connected with the armature B, through three elastic bars C, which provide the drive when the armature is attracted by the magnet.

The electric current which actuates the magnet is fed through a thermo-switch control screwed into either the cylinder head or the radiator.

When the cooling water temperature rises to approximately 185°F, the thermo-control switches on and the fan takes up the drive.

When the cooling water temperature drops, the thermo-control switches off at a much lower temperature and disengages the fan. The 18°F interval between on and off temperatures represent a sufficient time period to avoid too frequent switching on and off.

The electric current from the thermo-control D, reaches a carbon E, mounted on the water pump body, which bears on the insulated collector ring F, which, in turn, is connected to one end of the wire of the electromagnet coil G, the other end of which is earthed to the revolving mass. The current returns from the revolving earth to a solid earth through the water pump shaft, impeller and axially through the carbon of the seal to the water pump body.

4:2 Routine maintenance, fan belt tension

There is only one lubrication point and this is a nipple on the water pump casing which should be oiled with engine oil at every 1800 miles.

The cooling system should be drained, flushed through and refilled at regular intervals.

During very cold weather, anti-freeze should be added to the cooling system to prevent freezing. Before adding the anti-freeze mixture, the cooling system should be drained and flushed through with water until it runs out clean. Before refilling, check the condition of all hoses and connections in the cooling system and to the heater. Inspect the cylinder head to block and other

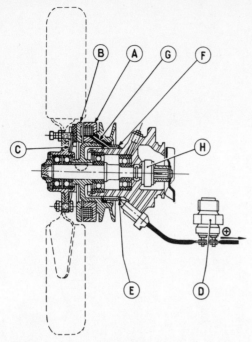

FIG 4:1   Cross-section of the magnetic clutch fan

Key to Fig 4:1   **A** Electro-magnet   **B** Armature
C Fan drive bars   **D** Thermo-switch control   **E** Carbon
brush   **F** Collector ring   **G** Electro-magnet coil   **H** Pump
seal

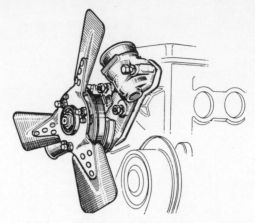

FIG 4:3   The water pump attached to engine

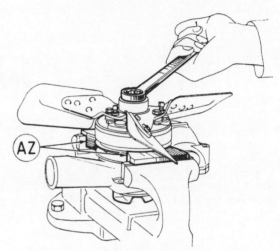

FIG 4:4   Removing the water pump centre nut

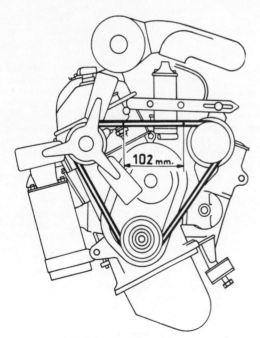

FIG 4:2   Fan belt adjustment

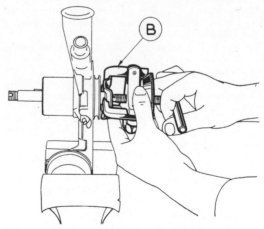

FIG 4:5   Removing the impeller

similar joints for leaks. It is advisable to mix the anti-freeze with water in a suitable container before filling the cooling system.

Fan belt tension:

The adjustment of the fan belt is based upon a calculated amount of stretch after fitting to the car. Before installing the fan belt, draw two pencil lines on the top surface of the belt, 100 mm (3.937 inch) apart.

After installing the belt, tension it so that the distance between the pencil marks, made before installation, does not exceed 102 mm (4.015 inch) (see **FIG 4:2**). The belt will appear to be loose by normal standards but it should not be tightened beyond this point unless it is slipping. Excessive tightness will cause the belt to wear very quickly and may damage the generator and water pump.

4:3 Water pump removal and installation

The location and mounting of the water pump and fan on the engine can be seen in **FIG 4:3**. To remove the pump proceed as follows:

1 Drain the cooling system and disconnect the battery.
2 Remove the fan belt and the top radiator hose.
3 Disconnect the lower water hose and the heater pipe.
4 Remove the electrical wire at the thermo-control switch and carbon holder or remove the carbon holder, according to the type of pump fitted.
5 Remove the five attachment screws and withdraw the pump from the engine.

To install the water pump, carefully clean the mating faces on the water pump and the cylinder head. Smear both faces of the new gasket with sealing compound and reverse the removal instructions.

4:4 Pump dismantling

1 Hold the pulley in a vice with soft jaws, unlock and remove the centre nut (see **FIG 4:4**). Hold the pulley by hand over a bench and strike the end of the shaft with a mallet to disengage the pulley and fan. Do not rest the pulley on the bronze collector ring. Remove the Woodruff key from the shaft.
2 Drive out the impeller securing pin, if fitted, and, using a suitable puller (see **FIG 4:5**), withdraw the impeller from the shaft.
3 Place a few drops of oil under the collar of the seal and rotate the puller C, from tool kit No. 8.0107Z (see **FIG 4:6**), in order to remove the seal. Remove the front bearing snap ring. Submerge the pump body in boiling water for about one minute, and then press out the shaft with its two bearings. The bearings can be removed from the shaft in a press.

Inspection and testing:

1 Check the condition of the bearings and seal assembly and renew them as necessary.
2 Test the electro-magnet winding as follows:

Using two test wire probes, one plain and one with an ammeter connected in series, attach the plain lead to the positive terminal of a 12-volt battery and the ammeter lead to the negative terminal of the battery (see **FIG 4:7**).

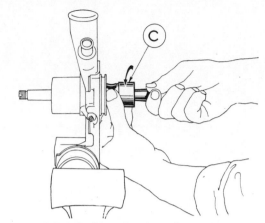

FIG 4:6   Removing the cyclam seal

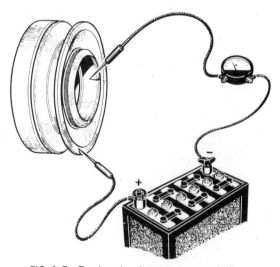

FIG 4:7   Testing the electro-magnet winding

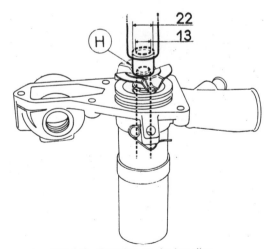

FIG 4:8   Pressing on the impeller

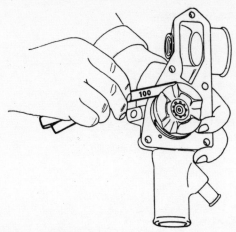

FIG 4:9 Checking the clearance between the front face of the impeller blades and the rear face of the water pump body

FIG 4:10 Exploded view showing the centre nut, fan, pulley and Woodruff key

Place the ammeter lead probe on the inside of the pulley collector ring and the probe of the plain lead on the pulley body. No reading on the ammeter will indicate an open circuit in the electro-magnet winding. •

A reading of .6 amps indicates that the winding is serviceable, while a reading of more than .6 amps indicates that there is a short circuit in the winding. The pulley assembly must be renewed if found to be unserviceable.

4:5 Pump reassembly

1 Grease the ballbearings with multi-purpose grease and press them onto the shaft with their open sides facing each other.
2 Heat the water pump body by immersing in boiling water for several minutes and press the shaft and bearing assembly into position in the body. Fit the retaining circlip in the recess in the front of the pump body.
3 Strike the rear end of the shaft to take up the play between the front bearing and the circlip.
4 Lubricate the rear end of the shaft and install a new seal.

5 Engage the impeller into the driving fingers of the seal and over the splines on the shaft. Press the impeller on gently with a bush (see FIG 4:8), having an inside diameter of $\frac{1}{2}$ inch (13 mm), and an outside diameter of $\frac{7}{8}$ inch (22 mm).
6 Adjust the position of the impeller, which must rotate without runout and with a maximum clearance of .04 inch (1 mm) between the blades and the pump collar (see FIG 4:9).
7 Drill and fit the impeller retaining pin, if originally fitted.
8 At the front end of the shaft, install the Woodruff key, the electro-magnet pulley, and the fan (see FIG 4:10).
9 Hold the pulley in a vice with protected jaws and install the nut and lockwasher and tighten to a torque of 21.6 to 28.9 lb ft.
10 Check the gap between the fan and the electro-magnet. This should be between .014 to .016 inch. If necessary, adjust this clearance by means of the three square headed screws and locknuts on the front face of the fan (see FIG 4:11). Check the gap at three positions adjacent to each screw.
On later cars this dimension is reduced to .012 inch.
11 Check the operation of the fan by connecting the carbon holder lead to the positive terminal and the pump body to the negative terminal of a battery.

4:6 Testing the thermo-switch

1 Start the engine and allow it to reach its normal operating temperature. The fan should take up the

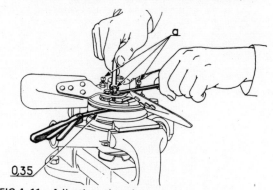

FIG 4:11 Adjusting the clearance between the fan armature and the electro-magnet

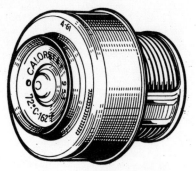

FIG 4:12 The thermostat

drive when the temperature of the cooling water reaches 185°F, and switch off again when the temperature of the water falls to 167°F.

2 If the fan fails to take up the drive at the specified temperature, check the fuse F3 under the dashboard.

3 If the fuse has not blown, bridge the terminals of the thermoswitch, located at the bottom of the radiator, with a jumper wire. If the fan now takes up the drive, the thermo-switch is faulty and should be renewed. The thermo-switch tightening torque is 21.6 to 36.1 lb ft.

Thermostat:

The thermostat plug on the exit side of the water pump prevents cold water from passing into the top tank of the radiator. The water is then recirculated through the engine until it is hot enough to open the thermostat valve, thus giving a quick warm up.

The thermostat can be tested by immersing it in water so that it does not touch the bottom or sides of the container. The temperature of the water is raised until the thermostat valve starts to open. If the valve does not open at the specified temperature, or sticks in the fully open position it must be renewed. It is not possible to repair a defective thermostat.

Two types of thermostat are manufactured and can be identified by a reference number and by the colouring. The thermostat for normal use is coloured red and numbered 951. The valve in this model starts to open at 72°C and is fully open at 80°C.

For 'deep frost' countries a thermostat reference 944 and coloured black is fitted. The valve in this model starts to open at 88°C and is fully open at 97°C. The thermostat is shown in **FIG 4:12.**

4:7 Fault diagnosis

(a) Internal water leakage

1 Cracked cylinder wall
2 Loose cylinder head nuts
3 Cracked cylinder head
4 Faulty head gasket
5 Cracked tappet chest wall

(b) Poor circulation

1 Radiator core blocked
2 Engine water passages restricted
3 Low water level
4 Loose fan belt
5 Defective thermostat
6 Perished or collapsed radiator hoses

(c) Corrosion

1 Impurities in the water
2 Infrequent draining and flushing

(d) Overheating

1 Check (b)
2 Sludge in crankcase
3 Faulty ignition timing
4 Low oil level in sump
5 Tight engine
6 Choked exhaust system
7 Binding brakes
8 Slipping clutch
9 Incorrect valve timing
10 Retarded ignition
11 Mixture too weak

NOTES

CHAPTER 5

THE CLUTCH

5:1 Description

The 404 has a conventional single dry plate clutch. Earlier cars had a Ferodo PKSC unit with 9 coil springs, as shown in section in **FIG 5:1**. From late 1967 this was replaced by a Ferodo 215D diaphragm spring clutch. The change does not affect servicing procedure.

Two types of driven plate disc are in service, the type fitted depending on the depth of the recess in the flywheel (see **FIG 5:2**). Consequently, the driven discs cannot be interchanged, but the flywheels may be interchanged provided the appropriate driven discs are fitted. All Peugeot 404 models from Serial Number 4.104.576 are fitted with flywheels with the 25.5 mm deep recess.

5:2 Maintenance

The clutch thrust bearing has a lubricating nipple above the clutch housing and 1 cc of engine lubricating oil must be added at every 3000 km or 1900 miles.

Originally the clutch pedal had a 'safety free' travel of 15 to 20 mm before declutching. This limit has now been raised to 30 to 35 mm and may be adjusted as follows. Refer to **FIG 5:3** and remove the soundproof cardboard panels on the lefthand side of the clutch pedal. Loosen the locknut 1, on the pedal adjusting screw. Screw in the rubber buffer 2, by approximately two turns and retighten the locknut. Re-install the soundproofing panel. Set the pedal free travel to 30 to 35 mm by turning the brass nut behind the master cylinder reservoir. Turn the nut clockwise to reduce the play and anticlockwise to increase.

5:3 Clutch control adjustment

From Peugeot 404 5.030.292 the clutch control has been strengthened by increasing the diameter of the clutch jackshaft 2 (see **FIG 5:4**) and the following method should be used to adjust.

1 Adjust to 162 mm (6.377 inches) the distance 'a' between the hollow pin face on the clutch housing end and the centre of the bronze bush screwed onto the shaft.

2 Adjust to 14 mm (.551 inches) the distance 'b' between the centre of the bronze bush and the conical washer outer face.

3 The conical washer must bear firmly against the rubber protecting pad as well as against the shoulder of the shaft.

Key to Fig 5:1 A Early coil spring type B Later
diaphragm spring type

Key A: 1 Pressure plate 2 Clutch plate 3 Thrust
bearing 4 Fork 5 Flywheel 6 Starter ring gear
7 Housing 8 Crankshaft 9 Drive shaft

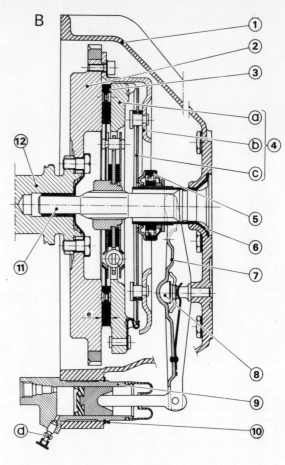

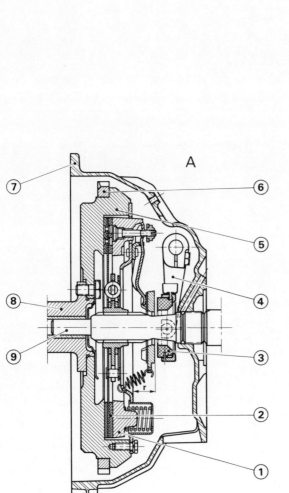

A

Key B: 1 Housing 2 Flywheel 3 Clutch plate
4a Pressure plate 4b Cover 4c Diaphragm 5 Ball
bearing 6 Guide bush 7 Fork 8 Fork thrust ball
9 Slave cylinder 10 Retaining clip 11 Drive shaft
12 Crankshaft

For all cars built prior to this modification the corresponding dimensions are:

a   161 mm (6.338 inches).
b   22 mm (.866 inches).

5:4 Removing the clutch

To remove the clutch and transmission it is not necessary to remove the engine but the rear axle and transmission must be removed as follows:

1 Disconnect the battery.
2 Install the engine support cross beam, No. 8.0116 In position as shown in **FIG 5:5**. Insert the rod into the suspension eyelet below the ignition coil and screw in a few turns to support the engine.
3 Remove the clutch thrust bearing lubricating tube and disconnect the thrust bearing linkage and return spring.
4 Remove the clutch housing plates and disconnect the speedometer cable.
5 Unscrew the two nuts from the clamp securing the exhaust pipe to the manifold, as well as the nut securing the clamp to the rear gearbox housing.
6 Disconnect the gearchange controls and the handbrake cables at the brake equalizer and floor connections.
7 Disconnect the hydraulic brake hose from its attachment lug and the flange securing the fuel and brake lines.
8 Remove the rear engine mounting attaching screws.
9 Disconnect the rear shock absorbers at the axle tube, and the stabilizer bar at the lefthand side.
10 Remove the screws securing the torque tube ball joint, jack up the rear of the car and disconnect the rear springs.
11 Move the rear axle rearwards to clear the torque tube at the universal joint splines.
12 Support the gearbox, remove the clutch housing retaining screws, withdraw the gearbox rearwards and remove from the car.
13 Mark the clutch mechanism in relation to the flywheel in order to facilitate correct reassembly. Slacken each of the six retaining bolts approximately one turn at a time, working diagonally across the clutch, until all the pressure has been removed from the coil springs or diaphragm.

5:5 Driven plate and pressure plate

Inspect the clutch disc and pressure plate. Check that the linings are secure and free from oil. The disc should also be checked for excessive wear and signs of overheating. If the linings are worn down near to the rivet heads, or, if any of the above conditions are present, the disc should be renewed.

Check the condition of the pressure plate and the release plate surface. Should any signs of scoring, overheating or distortion be present, change the assembly.

For inspection, removal and repair of the flywheel see **Section 1:9**.

5:6 Refitting the clutch

To refit the clutch assembly, align the marks on the flywheel and clutch cover made during dismantling, and install the clutch assembly using a used clutch shaft to align the driven plate with the clutch spigot.

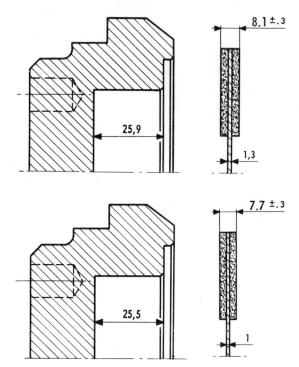

FIG 5:2   Dimensions of two types of driven disc (see Section 5:1)

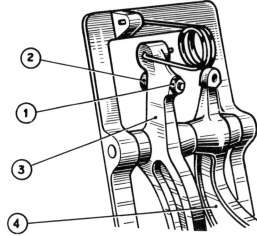

FIG 5:3   Clutch pedal adjustment screw

Key to Fig 5:3   1 Locknut   2 Rubber buffer

5:7 Electro-magnetic Jaeger coupler

On Peugeot 404J models an electro-magnetic Jaeger coupler is fitted to the flywheel. The circuit diagram for the system can be seen in **FIG 5:6**. The governor is a centrifugal switch fitted on the gearbox, driven by the output shaft. The governor opens at about 16 mile/hr while speed is increasing and closes at about 12.5 mile/hr when speed is decreasing, thus controlling the

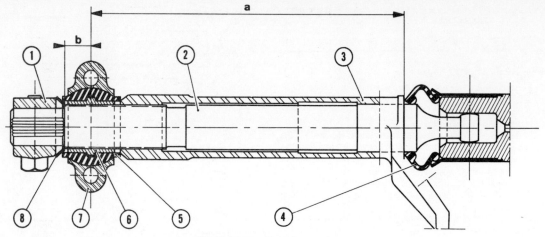

FIG 5:4   The clutch control

Key to Fig 5:4   1 Clutch jackshaft lever   2 Clutch jackshaft   3 Changespeed jackshaft   4 Rubber protector   5 Jackshaft bearing bushing   6 Sleeve   7 Bearing cap   8 Sealing washer

inner switch which is connected to the R1 relay of the control, which feeds the coupler either from the generator or the battery.

Coupler removal:

1 Disconnect the SUBAL (brush holder) and remove it from the side of the transmission casing (see **FIG 5:7**).

2 Remove the gearbox as detailed in **Section 5:4**.

3 Remove the six 6 mm Allen screws, but be sure to leave untouched the two opposed screws marked with yellow paint, arrowed in **FIG 5:8**.

4 Remove the coupler by hand, tapping with a mallet around the periphery if necessary.

5 Unscrew the six flywheel attachment screws, mark on the flywheel the distributor setting notch (see **FIG 5:8**), and remove the flywheel.

Introducing magnetic powder (New coupler):

Unscrew the non-painted plug with a Number 5 Allen key and hold the coupler vertically.

Drop the whole of a bag of magnetic powder into the coupler using a non-metallic funnel. Use a drive shaft to rotate the polepiece to evenly distribute the powder. Clean the thread and replace the plug. Once filled with powder the coupler must be kept in a vertical position.

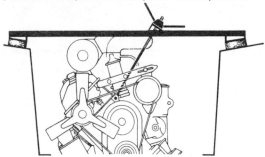

FIG 5:5   Engine support beam in position for clutch removal

Exchanging powder on original coupler:

Unscrew on the side of the flywheel the 8 screws with cross-shaped slots in the head, and remove the coupler lid (see **FIG 5:9**).

Take out the removable armature and the whole of the powder. Clean the inside of the coupler with a clean dry brush. Replace the armature and the lid and refit the 8 screws. Refill the coupler with powder in the same way as for a new coupler described previously.

Starter crownwheel replacement:

The coupler should be placed on wooden blocks to prevent damage to the terminals of the collector rings. Strike around the crownwheel, using a bronze drift and a hammer until the ring is completely released. To fit a new crownwheel it should first be gently heated with a blowlamp. Place it over the flywheel and coupler and tap into place while still warm.

5:8   Refitting the coupler

1 Install the flywheel, paired with the coupler, onto the crankshaft. Ensure that the marks on the flywheel made during removal are aligned with the distributor setting notch.

2 Replace the flywheel attachment screws and torque load them to 43.7 lb ft.

3 Place the coupler over the flywheel, ensuring that it is correctly located on its two location studs. Replace the six attachment screws and lockwashers and torque load to 7.2 lb ft.

4 Refit the gearbox and referring to **FIG 5:7**, install the Subal. Use a thin blade to hold the 4 carbons into their housings. Refit the Subal electrical wires.

5:9   Accelerator cable replacement

1 Remove the central panel from under the dashboard.

2 Disconnect the cable from the accelerator pedal.

GENERATOR

BATTERY

7 circuit closer

M

3rd brush

92

7

4 1 - 21

20

main switch

2

COIL
95

3

Distributor

F6
generator fuse
18 A

F5
battery fuse
18 A

Fuses plate and
emergency connexions

92

82

95

88

94

94

80

93

90

GOVERNOR

generator
battery relay
R1

88

87

82

Economy
resistor

91

91

87

CONAC

89

Slow running
resistor

86

86

89

93

Clutch on

80

83 83

81

81

COUPLER

Clutch off

Demagnet
resistor

84

84

POGEL

R2 Coupler control

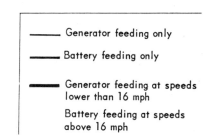

Generator feeding only

Battery feeding only

Generator feeding at speeds
lower than 16 mph

Battery feeding at speeds
above 16 mph

FIG 5:6   Jaeger coupling electrical circuit. POGEL is the manual override control

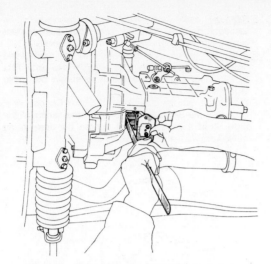

FIG 5:7   Removing and replacing the Subal

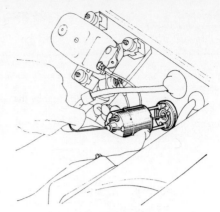

FIG 5:10   Removing Conac

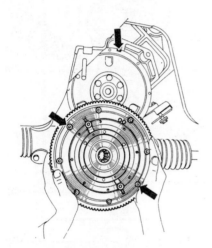

FIG 5:8   Removing the Jaeger coupling

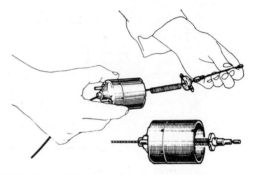

FIG 5:11   Refitting accelerator cable and spring to Conac

FIG 5:9   Coupling with lid and armature removed

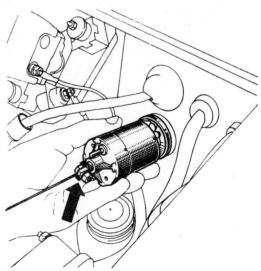

FIG 5:12   Refitting the Conac

3 Disconnect the cable from the carburetter and remove the sheath.
4 Disconnect the electrical wires from the Conac (accelerator cable double switch).
5 Remove the Conac assembling nuts which also act as connection terminals, but do not remove the rubber washers from the studs.
6 Remove the cable and Conac, holding it by the centre piece (see **FIG 5:10**).
7 Replace the cable, the spring and the connection in the order shown in **FIG 5:11**.

8 Pull the cable until the contact comes into its location grooves, making sure that the contact resting spring is correctly fitted into its recesses.
.9 Bring the switch into the bottom of the casing and hold it in this position with a cable clip (see **FIG 5:12**). Care must be taken not to distort the cable with the clip.
10 Install the whole assembly onto the Conac base, engaging the cable arrester through the centre of the base. Refit the washers and tighten the assembling nuts. Remove the cable clip.

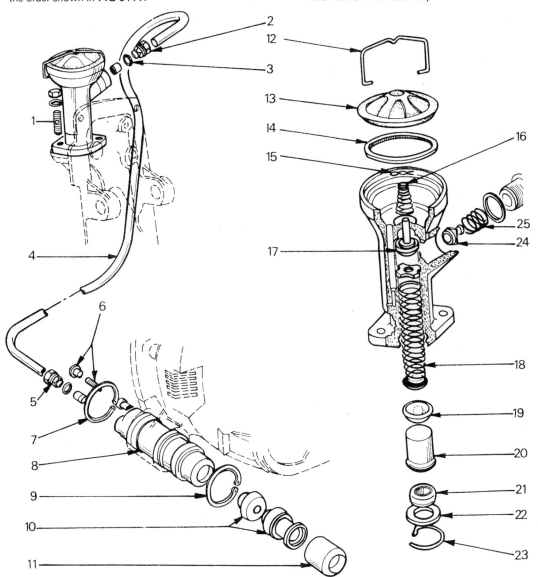

FIG 5:13   Components of hydraulic clutch operation

Key to Fig 5:13   1 Fixing bolt or stud   2 Union nut   3 Washer   4 Fluid supply pipe   5 Union nut   6 Bleed screw and cover
7 Front circlip   8 Slave cylinder   9 Rear circlip   10 Piston assembly   11 Rubber boot   12 Wire clip   13 Top cover
14 Gasket   15 Spring clip   16 Spring   17 Supply valve   18 Conical spring   19 Secondary cup   20 Piston   21 Primary cup
22 Washer   23 Circlip   24 Valve   25 Spring

11 Reconnect the electrical wires.
12 Reconnect the cable to the accelerator pedal. Install a new sheath on the carburetter end of the cable and install the adjustment shim between the sheath and the carburetter before connecting the cable to the accelerator control lever.

5:10 Hydraulic clutch operation

From 1968 the clutch is operated by the hydraulic system illustrated in **FIG 5:13**. As will be seen, this consists of a master cylinder, operated directly by the clutch pedal and having an integral fluid reservoir and a slave cylinder mounted on the clutch housing and operating directly on the end of the clutch fork lever.

As the master cylinder incorporates a valve which maintains a residual pressure in the circuit no means of adjustment are provided and the free play at the clutch is nil.

Master cylinder:

This can be removed without disturbing the pedal. After taking steps to avoid fluid leakage, disconnect the fluid supply pipe as shown and then remove the two securing bolts.

Remove the wire clip and lift off the top cover and gasket. Extract the spring clip on the supply valve.

Remove the circlip and washer, then withdraw the piston and the secondary cup followed by the primary cup, spring and supply valve.

Reassembly is a reversal of the above procedure, being careful to see that the wider end of the return spring is at the inner end of the cylinder.

Slave cylinder:

To remove the slave cylinder, remove the rear securing circlip on the clutch casing and pull the cylinder out towards the front. The piston operating rod remains attached to the clutch fork lever.

The components of the slave cylinder are clearly shown in the illustration and may be lifted out for inspection after removing the rubber boot.

When refitting the slave cylinder see that the bleed screw is on the bottom and then bleed the system.

It should not be necessary to mention that strict cleanliness must be observed when handling these parts as with all hydraulic systems.

Bleeding:

Raise the front of the car or run it over a pit and ensure that the fluid reservoir is full.

Attach a rubber tube to the bleed nipple and immerse its other end in a clean glass jar containing a quantity of clean brake fluid. Unscrew the bleed screw.

Have an assistant to operate fully the clutch pedal a few times, noting that at first there will be air bubbles in the fluid expelled into the jar. As soon as the fluid emerges free from any bubbles, tighten up the bleed screw, take off the rubber tube and replace the protecting cap.

Top up the reservoir to within $\frac{1}{4}$ inch of the cover joint face. The recommended fluid is Lockheed 55.

5:11 Clutch fault diagnosis

(a) Drag or spin

1 Oil or grease on driven plate linings
2 Misalignment between the engine and the main drive pinion
3 Driven plate hub binding on main drive pinion splines
4 Binding of main drive pinion bearing
5 Distorted clutch plate
6 Warped or damaged pressure plate or clutch cover
7 Broken driven plate linings
8 Dirt or foreign matter in clutch

(b) Fierceness or snatch

1 Check 1 and 2 in (a)
2 Worn clutch linings

(c) Slip

1 Check 1 in (a)
2 Check 2 in (b)
3 Weak pressure springs

(d) Judder

1 Check 1 and 2 in (a)
2 Pressure plate not parallel with flywheel face
3 Contact area of driven plate linings not evenly distributed
4 Bent first motion shaft
5 Buckled driven plate
6 Faulty engine or gearbox rubber mountings
7 Worn suspension
8 Weak rear springs

(e) Rattle

1 Check 3 in (c)
2 Broken springs in driven plate
3 Worn release mechanism
4 Excessive backlash in transmission
5 Wear in transmission bearings
6 Release bearing loose on fork

(f) Tick or knock

1 Worn first motion shaft spigot or bearing
2 Badly worn splines in driven plate hub
3 Release plate out of line
4 Faulty drive on starter motor
5 Loose flywheel

(g) Driven plate fracture

1 Check 2 in (a)
2 Drag and distortion due to hanging gearbox in plate hub

CHAPTER 6

THE GEARBOX OR TRANSMISSION

6:1 Description

Two types of gearbox have been fitted to the Peugeot 404 in the period covered by this manual, and it will be convenient to deal with them separately as there are some differences in the servicing procedures.

Type C3 is fitted to early cars, while type BA7 will be found on cars produced after 1967. Both boxes have four forward speeds and reverse, and all forward gears are synchronized. **FIG 6:1** shows a cutaway diagram of the early gearbox and the later type is shown in **FIG 6:2**.

In each case gear selection is by means of a lever operated mechanism mounted on the steering column. Details of gear reduction ratios will be found in Technical Data in the Appendix.

Routine maintenance:

Check the level of the oil in the gearbox at 1800 miles and drain and refill the gearbox every 3600 miles.

To check the oil level in the gearbox the car must be standing on level ground. Remove the oil level plug from the lefthand side of the transmission casing and the oil should be level with the bottom of the threaded hole.

When draining and refilling, remove both the level and drain plugs. When the gearbox is empty, replace the drain plug and fill the gearbox with oil until it runs out of the level plug. When the overflow has ceased, replace the level plug securely.

6:3 Removing the gearbox

Before commencing operations, disconnect the battery and place suitable covers over the wings.

Fit an engine support beam 8.0116 Y or other suitable lifting tackle to take the weight of the engine.

Remove the starter motor.

C3. Remove the clutch thrust bearing lubricating tube and disconnect the bearing linkage and return spring.

BA7. Remove the gear change jack shaft.

Separate the steering gearbox from the chassis cross-member and turn the steering wheel so as to move the steering column over towards the left.

Remove the clutch housing plates and the exhaust pipe at the manifold and from the clamp at the rear of the gearbox.

Withdraw the gear change control rods from the ball joints and then disconnect the speedometer drive, the handbrake control cables at both the equalizer and the floor connections and also the hydraulic brake hose from its attachment ring. Remove the clamp securing the fuel and brake pipes.

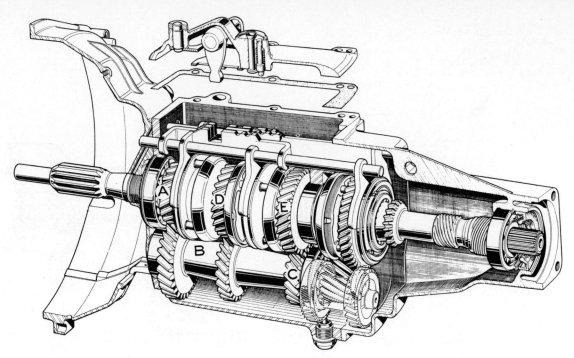

FIG 6:1 Sectioned view of the C3 type gearbox

Key to Fig 6:1   **A** Main drive gear   **B** 3rd speed countershaft gear   **C** 2nd speed countershaft gear   **D** 3rd speed synchronizer gear   **E** 2nd speed synchronizer gear

BA7. Remove the rear retaining ring from the clutch slave cylinder.

Place a suitable support under the gearbox and then remove the engine rear mounting bolts.

Disconnect the rear dampers from the axle tubes and the stabilizer bar from the lefthand axle tube.

If thermostable brakes are fitted the compensator spring must be detached from the stabilizer, but do not slacken the nut securing the clamp spring assembly.

Disconnect the rear anti-roll bar from the connecting links and remove the four bolts securing the torque tube ball joint. Note that it may be necessary to free the body to gain access to the two upper bolts.

Jack up the rear end of the car and remove the rear springs.

Move the rear axle assembly toward the rear to clear the torque tube at the universal joint splines.

Remove the rear engine mounting and the clutch operating rod. Remove three Allen screws securing the clutch housing and withdraw the gearbox to the rear.

On BA7 gearboxes the slave cylinder should be removed from the front, it is not necessary to disconnect the hydraulic pipe.

Refitting the gearbox:

This is carried out by reversing the removal procedure, paying attention to the following points:

In order to ensure the alignment of the gearbox, the front cross piece support must be slackened before recoupling the differential.

Do not rely on hand support only, use a suitable lifting tackle under the clutch housing.

Use new Nylstop nuts when refitting the rear dampers.

6:4 Gearbox dismantling

1 Remove the oil level and drain plugs and drain the gearbox.
2 Remove the clutch housing and gearbox top cover (see **FIG 6:4**).
3 Select two gears, remove the universal joint attaching screw and withdraw the universal joint.
4 Remove the speedometer drive assembly from the lefthand side of the rear extension.
5 Remove the rear extension housing retaining nuts and washers and withdraw the extension housing.
6 Remove the rear oil seal, bronze washer and rear bearing from the rear extension housing.
7 Remove the adjusting shims and speedometer drive worm from the mainshaft.
8 Extract the reverse gearshaft lock screw and remove the shaft, reverse idler and gear and washers (see **FIG 6:5**).
9 Remove the selector shafts and forks. The selector shafts are removed towards the front of the gearbox.
10 Withdraw the main drive gear from the front of the gearbox.
11 Maintain two gears in engagement, unlock and remove the nut on the front of the mainshaft. Unlock and remove the nut from the rear end of the countershaft and withdraw the 1st speed gear.

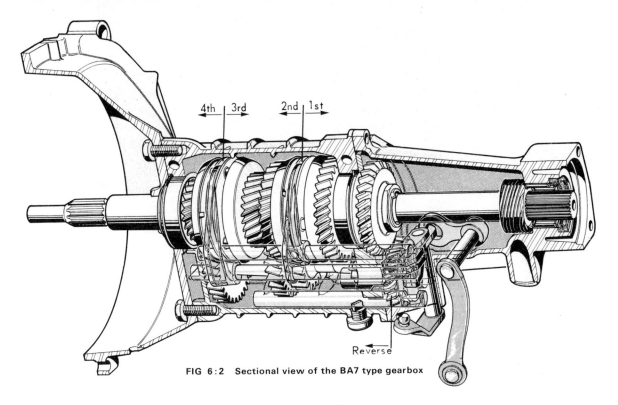

FIG 6:2 Sectional view of the BA7 type gearbox

12 Using a mallet, drive the mainshaft carefully out to the rear of the gearbox, collecting the components as they become free in the following order: 4th speed synchronizer and cone, 3rd speed gear and bushing, 2nd and 3rd speed synchronizer and hub and 2nd speed gear. The mainshaft and its components can be seen in **FIG 6:6.**

Note that the mainshaft will come out with the 2nd speed gear shoulder bushing, centre bearing and 1st speed synchronizer cone in place. For further stripping see under Dismantling Mainshaft.

13 Remove the countershaft rear bearing snap ring, push the countershaft towards the rear of the gearbox and, using a suitable puller, withdraw the rear bearing.

14 Push the countershaft and front bearing to the rear of the gearbox to free the bearing and withdraw the assembly through the top opening of the gearbox.

15 If the selector control on the lefthand side of the gearbox is to be removed, it will be necessary to mark the lower lever on the shaft splines to ensure correct reassembly. Failure to observe this precaution will result in incorrect gear engagement on reassembly. When the control is correctly assembled (see **FIG 6:7**), the upper lever should point rearwards parallel to the gearbox centre line and the lower lever at approximately 59 deg. outwards.

Dismantling the main drive gear:

1 Hold the main drive gear in a vice with protected jaws.
2 Unlock and remove the bearing retaining nut from the shaft (see **FIG 6:8**). Note that the nut has a lefthand thread.

3 Remove the snap ring from the outer race of the bearing and, using a suitable puller, withdraw the bearing from the shaft.
4 Remove the oil deflector washer noting the way the offset of the washer is fitted.

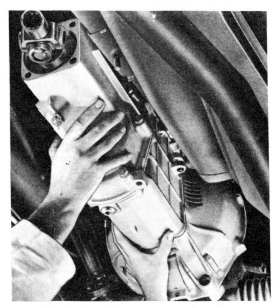

FIG 6:3 Removing the gearbox from the car

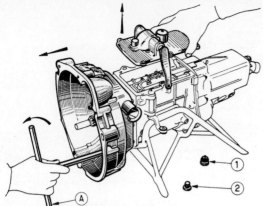

FIG 6:4 Removing gearbox top cover and clutch housing

Key to Fig 6:4   1 Oil level plug   2 Drain plug

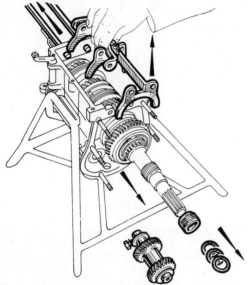

FIG 6:5 Removing reverse gear spindle and idler, and selector fork

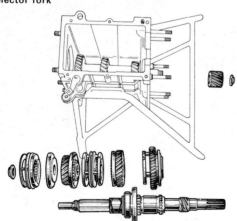

FIG 6:6 The mainshaft and its components

Reassembling the main drive gear:

1 Install the oil deflector washer on the drive gear shaft and press on the bearing with the snap ring groove towards the outside.

2 Install the retaining nut and tighten to a torque of 45 to 60 lb ft.

3 Stake the nut and fit the snap ring to the groove in the bearing outer race. Retain the drive gear for later installation.

Dismantling the mainshaft:

1 Remove the 2nd speed gear bushing and extract the stop pin (see **FIG 6:9**).

2 Using a suitable puller, withdraw the bearing from the shaft.

3 Remove the 1st speed synchronizing cone.

Reassembling the mainshaft:

1 Install the 1st speed synchronizer cone on the mainshaft and fit the intermediate bearing to abut the synchronizer cone. Make sure that the 2nd speed gear bushing stop pin hole is completely exposed.

2 Fit the stop pin and install the 2nd speed gear bushing to engage the stop pin in the appropriate recess in the bushing. Retain the mainshaft for later installation.

The countershaft gear:

Gearboxes with an A or B prefix to the serial number have built up countershafts and the countershaft is dismantled as set out below. Gearboxes with the prefix C to the serial number indicates that the countershaft gears are of one piece and dismantling comprises only of removing the bearing and thrust washer.

To dismantle a countershaft from a gearbox prefixed A or B, hold the countershaft in a vice fitted with protected jaws, unlock and remove the front nut.

Remove the 3rd speed constant mesh gear and bearing from the 2nd speed constant mesh gear shaft.

Reassemble the countershaft by reversing the dismantling procedure.

6:5 Reassembling the gearbox

1 Before starting to reassemble the gearbox ensure that all parts are clean. Oil the parts with gear oil during

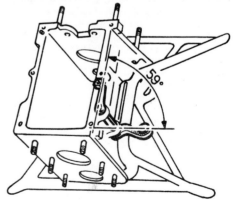

FIG 6:7 Correct configuration of selector control levers

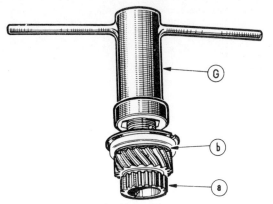

FIG 6:8   Main drive gear

Key to Fig 6:8   **a** 4th speed gear   **b** Oil deflector washer   **G** Spanner

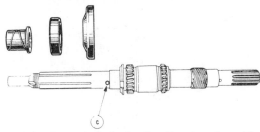

FIG 6:9   The mainshaft showing the stop pin **c**. Dismantled from the shaft is the 2nd speed gear flanged bushing, the intermediate ballbearing and the 1st speed synchronizer

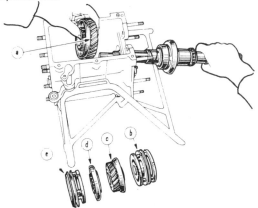

FIG 6:10   Installing the mainshaft in the gearbox case

Key to Fig 6:10   **a** 2nd speed gear   **b** 2nd/3rd speed synchronizer and hub   **c** 3rd speed synchronizer gear and bushing   **d** 4th speed synchronizer cone   **e** 4th speed synchronizer

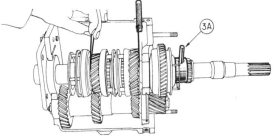

FIG 6:11   Checking the clearance between 2nd speed gear and bushing flange, and between 3rd and 4th speed gears. The special tool 3A is used to retain 1st speed gear in engagement

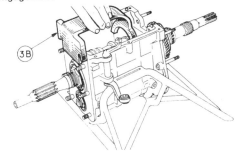

FIG 6:12   Fitting the special gauge 3B

reassembly and always fit new gaskets. Wash the bearings in clean solvent and blow dry. Do not spin the bearings with compressed air or they will be damaged. After a thorough cleaning, lubricate the bearings with light engine oil to prevent rusting. Turn the lubricated bearings slowly through your fingers to feel for roughness and excessive play.

Wash the transmission, clutch and transmission case with cleaning solvent and blow dry. Inspect the case for cracks or burrs which might hinder the proper seating of a snap ring. Dress off any burrs with a fine cut file.

Clean the gears thoroughly and replace any that are worn or damaged.

Check the bushings in the case for excessive wear. Check the synchronizer cones for wear or looseness in the clutches. If the cones are damaged in any way it will be necessary to renew the clutch assembly and rings.

2 Insert the countershaft through the top opening of the gearbox case and position it with the front bearing in its recess.

3 Turn the case on its front end with the front end of the countershaft resting on a wooden block and drift on the rear bearing.

4 Install the 1st speed gear on the countershaft and fit a new nut finger tight.

5 Enter the mainshaft, partly assembled as detailed in the previous Section, in the rear opening of the gear case and complete the assembly in the following order (see **FIG 6:10**).

2nd speed gear with the plain side to bearing.
2nd and 3rd synchronizer and hub.
3rd speed gear and bushing.
4th speed cone and synchronizer.

6 Push the mainshaft assembly towards the front of the gear case to engage the intermediate bearing in its boss in the case. Fit a new nut to the front of the mainshaft and tighten finger tight.

7 Install the 1st/reverse sliding gear and synchronizer on the rear end of the main shaft.

8 Engage and hold in two gears, 1st and 2nd speeds. Tighten the nut on the rear end of the countershaft and torque load to 45 to 50 lb ft. Lock the nut by

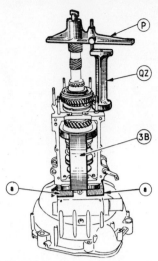

FIG 6:13 Assessing shim thickness required between rear housing bearing and speedometer drive gear

FIG 6:14 Rear housing extension

Key to Fig 6:14   a Oil seal   b Rear bearing snap ring
c Bearing end float shim   d Rear ballbearing

staking to the shaft. Tighten the nut on the front end of the main shaft and torque load to 15 to 22 lb ft.

9 Hold the main shaft in its correct position and check the clearance between the 2nd speed gear and the gear bushing shoulder (see **FIG 6:11**). Then check the clearance between the 3rd speed gear and 4th speed main gear. The clearance in each case should be .012 to .024 inch. If the clearance is correct in each case, lock the mainshaft nut by staking it to the main shaft.

10 Install the main drive gear, assembled as detailed in **Section 6:4,** and tap it into position until the snap ring is bottomed in its recess.

11 Install the special gauge 3B (see **FIG 6:12**) and attach it to the gearbox front face by the two top nuts. With the gearbox in neutral, the gauge fork should fit into the 2nd speed synchronizer and the 2nd speed cone should rest on it when the gearbox is placed vertically, rear end uppermost as shown in **FIG 6:13.**

12 Install the gearbox rear bearing in its recess in the rear extension housing (see **FIG 6:14**), and fit the retaining snap ring.

13 Measure the end float of the bearing in its recess and fit shims between the bearing and the snap ring to reduce the end float to zero. Shims are available for service in the following sizes: .075 inch, .079 inch and .083 inch.

14 Install the rear oil seal.

15 Lay the clutch housing front face down on a bench and place the gearbox upright on the housing using $\frac{3}{4}$ inch wooden blocks between the box and the housing either side of the main drive gear (see **FIG 6:13**).

16 Make sure that the 2nd speed synchronizer cone is firmly seated against the gauge 3B and install the speedometer drive gear on the main shaft.

17 Install the special gauge P in position and hold it firmly by means of its setscrew (see **FIG 6:13**). With the block QZ in position on the rear face of the gearbox, bring the gauge rod into contact with the gauge block and lock with the thumb screw.

18 Stand the gearbox rear extension housing on its rear end and transfer the block QZ and the gauge P to the extension housing as shown in **FIG 6:15.** The distance between the rod and the block determines

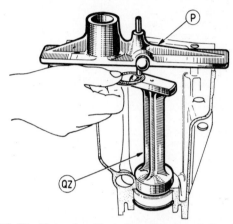

FIG 6:15 Measuring block QZ and gauge P fitted to rear extension housing. The gap between the end of the rod of gauge P and the top of the block QZ is the thickness of shims required between the rear bearing and the speedometer drive gear

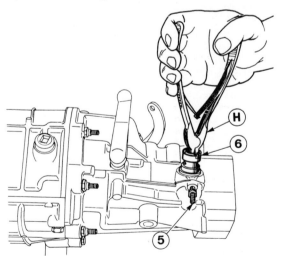

FIG 6:16 Removing the speedometer drive socket

Key to Fig 6:16   5 Stop screw   6 Drive socket   H Pliers

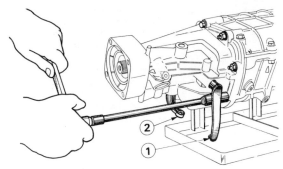

FIG 6:17   Removing the rear housing

Key to 6:17   1 Control lever   2 Selector lever

the shim thickness to be inserted between the rear extension housing bearing and the speedometer drive gear on the mainshaft in order to maintain correct adjustment.

19 Install the reverse idler gear, washers and shaft and secure the shaft with its lockscrew.

20 Place the gearbox in a horizontal position and remove the gauge fork 3B. Install the selector shafts and forks and the clutch housing using a new gasket. Check that the assembly turns freely when turned by hand and position the locating rings on the rear face of the gearbox housing.

21 Install the shims, determined in operation 18, on the mainshaft against the speedometer drive gear, coat the face of the rear extension housing with sealing cement, and install the housing, tightening the attaching nuts to a torque load of 12.5 to 18 lb ft.

22 Install the universal joint and bronze bushing, engage two gears and tighten the attachment screw to a torque loading of 50 lb ft. Lock the screw by staking.

23 Install the gearbox top cover and gasket, using sealing cement, and check the operation of the gearbox through all gears.

24 Fill the gearbox with 2 pints of SAE.40 oil.

6:6 Dismantling the BA7 gearbox

Having removed the gearbox from the car and drained out all the oil, dismantling will be facilitated if it can be mounted on a suitable support base or stand.

Remove the clutch release fork and the clutch housing as described in **Chapter 5**, then remove the reverse lamp switch, stop screw (5 in **FIG 6:16**) and speedometer drive socket 6 using the special pliers H.

Release the attachment screw and remove the universal joint.

Reverse the position of the gearbox, see **FIG 6:17** set the control lever 1 to neutral and pull the selector lever 2 fully to the rear. Remove all seven bolts attaching the housing with a 13 mm long socket tool as shown. The rear housing may now be removed, tapping it with a mallet if necessary.

Refer to **FIG 6:18** and remove the four Allen head screws 3, then the eight screws from the half housings and lift off the upper housing. The complete gear and pinion assembly may now be withdrawn, but it is recom-

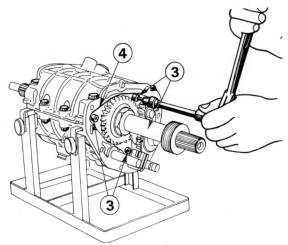

FIG 6:18   Removing the half housing

Key to Fig 6:18   3 Allen screws   4 Bearing lockplate

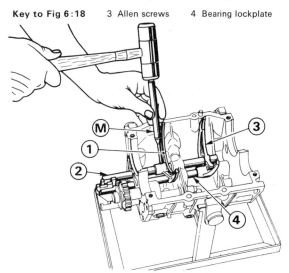

FIG 6:19   Removing the shifting forks

Key to Fig 6:19   1 1st/2nd gear fork   2 Fork shaft
3 3rd/4th gear fork   4 Fork shaft   M Drift

mended that any servicing should be entrusted to a service station.

To dismantle the shifting forks and locking devices, proceed as follows:

Engage second gear and remove the pin from the 1st/2nd gear shifting fork 1 as shown in **FIG 6:19**.

Engage fourth gear and remove the pin from the 3rd/4th gear shifting fork 3.

Refer to **FIG 6:20** and remove the locking plug 5 with a 5 mm Allen key and withdraw the 1st/2nd gear fork shaft 2 and the 3rd/4th gear shaft 4.

Refer to **FIG 6:21** and remove the locking plug 6 on the side of the gearbox to remove the reverse striking fork 7 with the counter shaft pinion.

Remove the three locking springs, four balls and the locking finger as shown in **FIG 6:22**. A 7 mm diameter rod may be used to free them if the balls get stuck in the channel.

Refer to **FIG 6:23** and remove the locking needle 1 from the 3rd/4th gear fork shaft.

Drive out the spiral pin, 2 in **FIG 6:24**, with a drift M from the reverse pinion shaft 3 and force this shaft towards the inside of the housing.

All the parts should now be thoroughly cleaned and oil drillings checked to ensure that they are free from obstruction.

Examine the splines the gear teeth for wear and also the friction surfaces of the synchronizing rings, comparing them with new parts if possible.

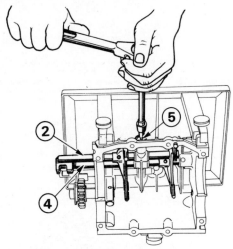

FIG 6:20   Removing the locking plug

Key to Fig 6:20   2 1st/2nd gear fork shaft   4 3rd/4th gear fork shaft   5 Locking plug

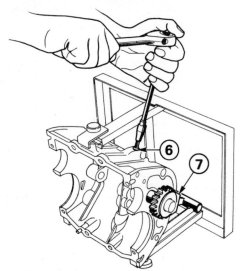

FIG 6:21   Removing the reverse shifting fork

Key to Fig 6:21   6 Locking plug   7 Shifting fork and countershaft pinion

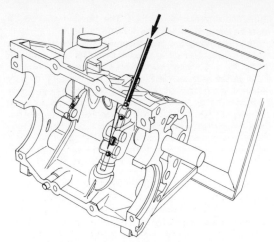

FIG 6:22   Locking springs and balls

Renew any defective parts, obtaining the help of the service station if necessary. It is advisable to renew the following parts whenever they are dismantled: snap rings, spring washers and striking fork pins, the mainshaft nut and oil seal. This latter is removed by prising out with a tyre lever, but needs a press for refitting. Any other seals or non-metallic washers should also be renewed. Dip all the components in clean engine oil before assembly.

6:7 Assembling the BA7 gearbox

Position the gearbox as in **FIG 6:25** with the drain hole uppermost and fit the reverse gear pinion and shifting fork in the direction shown, then insert the locking ball and spring into the channel shown in **FIG 6:26**. Secure with the plug after smearing the threads with sealer and tighten to a torque of 7.2 lb ft. Move the shifting fork shaft into the neutral position.

Turn the casing into the position shown in **FIG 6:27** with the locking channel 1 vertical and fit the 3rd/4th and reverse locking finger 2.

Smear a locking needle with tallow and fit it into its housing in the 3rd/4th gear charge fork shaft as shown in **FIG 6:23**.

Now turn the casing upright as in **FIG 6:28** and fit the two gear change forks in the order shown. That for the 1st/2nd gear is the larger (item 5) and is on the right and the smaller (item 6) for the 3rd/4th gear is on the left. Insert the fork shaft 4 until it is just flush with the ball lock hole 7.

Insert a spring and locking ball into the channel 1 in **FIG 6:29**, press the ball down with a drift M and then push the shaft 2 against the drift and withdraw the drift without releasing the pressure on the shaft.

Refer to **FIG 6:30**, move the shaft into the neutral position and secure the 3rd/4th fork 3 with a new locking pin.

Roll the casing on to its righthand side (**FIG 6:31**) and insert a locking ball into the passage 4 so as to rest against the 3rd/4th gear shaft 2. Insert the 1st/2nd gear shaft 5 until the neutral position is reached and then fit the locking ball 6 and spring 7 into passage 4. Secure with the plug 8 after applying a sealer to the threads and tighten to a torque of 7.2 lb ft. The 1st/2nd gear fork 9 must be secured with a new locking pin.

Before refitting the gear assembly the clutch housing must be checked for the parallelism of its front and rear faces. This is done by laying it on a flat surface and using a dial gauge as shown in **FIG 6:32**. The housing must be renewed of the faces are out of parallel by more than .1 mm.

Install the gear assembly into the lefthand housing as shown in **FIG 6:33**, taking care to see that the striking forks are correctly engaged with the synchronizer rings. Fit the outer race for the intermediate gearshaft front bearing if it was removed, then apply a thin coat of sealer to the mating faces of the half housings and fit them together.

Insert the four housing bolts shown at 4 in **FIG 6:34** and tighten them to a torque of 3.6 lb ft. Smear the rear face of the clutch housing with sealer and secure with six bolts tightened to 20 lb ft. Secure the rear backing plate with four Allen screws tightened to 7.2 lb ft.

Now slacken off the four housing bolts and tap the housing halves with a mallet while rotating the drive shaft. Finally retighten the four bolts to a torque of 11 lb ft.

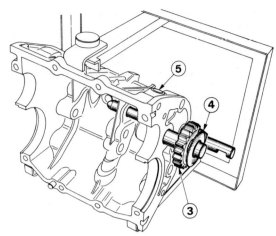

FIG 6:25   Fitting reverse pinion and fork

Key to Fig 6:25   3 Reverse gear   4 Shifting fork
5 Drain hole

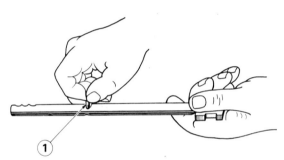

FIG 6:23   Removing the locking needle 1 from the 3rd/4th gear fork shaft

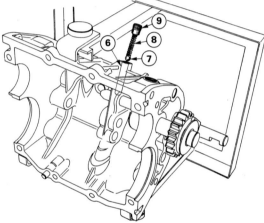

FIG 6:26   Installing the locking ball 7 and spring 8 in the channel 6 with plug 9

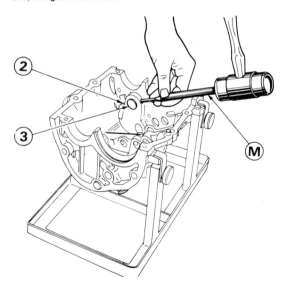

FIG 6:24   Removing the spiral pin 2 from the reverse pinion shaft 3

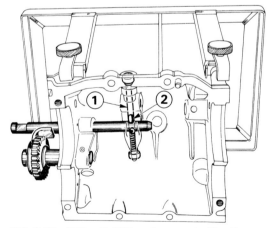

FIG 6:27   Fitting 3rd/4th and reverse locking finger

Key to Fig 6:27   1 Locking channel   2 Finger

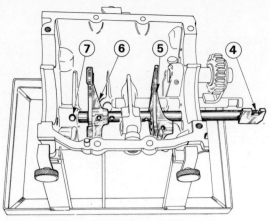

FIG 6:28 Fitting the shifting forks

Key to Fig 6:28   4 Shaft   5 1st/2nd gear fork   6 3rd/4th gear fork   7 Ball lock hole

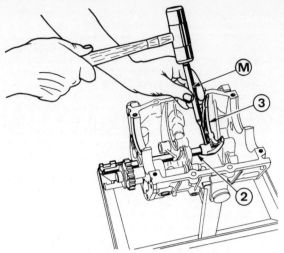

FIG 6:30 Securing 3rd/4th gear fork

Key to Fig 6:30   2 Shaft   3 Fork   M Drift

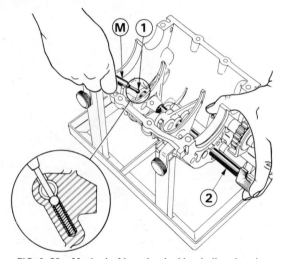

FIG 6:29 Method of locating locking ball and spring

Key to Fig 6:29   1 Channel   2 Shaft   M Drift

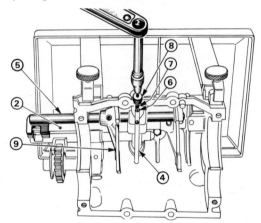

FIG 6:31 Fitting locking balls and springs

Key to Fig 6:31   2 3rd/4th gear shaft   4 Channel   5 1st/2nd gear shaft   6 Ball   7 Spring   8 Plug   9 1st/2nd gear fork

Refer to **FIG 6:35** for checking the out of level of the half housings at their rear mating surfaces. Using a dial indicator and support F as shown, the maximum out of flush is .02 mm. Install the four securing bolts 8 nuts and tighten to 7.2 lb ft, then smear the mating surface of the rear housing with sealer and fit the housing in position.

Engage the three double thread studs 1 and the four bolts 2 seen in **FIG 6:36,** pull the selector lever 3 fully backwards and tighten the seven studs and bolts to a torque of 11 lb ft. Oil the bearing in the rear housing.

Fit the speedometer drive socket with a new O-ring smeared with tallow and using the special pliers shown in **FIG 6:16** to rotate the parts into correct engagement. Fit the drive socket stop screw and its locknut.

Next fit the clutch release fork as described in **Chapter 5,** inserting the rubber cup filled with grease behind the ball thrust. The guide sleeve should have a smear of grease applied and the reverse lamp switch should have a new seal. Switches with a copper body and metal/plastic gaskets are tightened to 9 lb ft, but those with steel bodies and copper gaskets are tightened to 20 lb ft.

6:8 ZF automatic transmission

As an optional extra Peugeot 404 cars may be equipped with ZF automatic transmission system. It follows conventional lines in that it consists of a hydraulic torque converter coupled to the engine crankshaft by a flexible plate and an epicyclic gearbox giving three

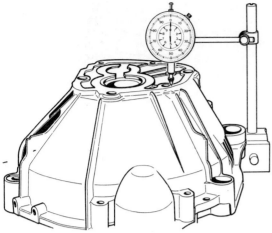

FIG 6:32 Checking alignment of clutch housing faces

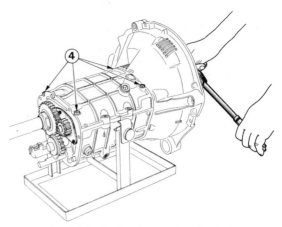

FIG 6:34 Fitting the gear housing bolts

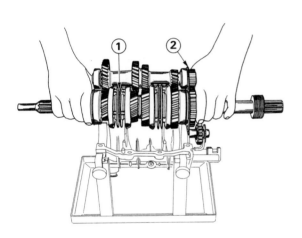

FIG 6:33 Refitting the gear assembly

Key to Fig 6:33   1 3rd/4th gear in neutral   2 Backing plate

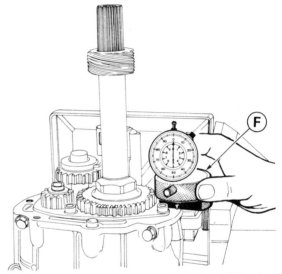

FIG 6:35 Checking the accuracy of the half housing fitting

forward speeds and reverse. Owing to the torque multiplication available there is a smooth progression through the ratios from rest to maximum speed.

A selector lever and indicating quadrant are mounted on the steering column by means of which the driver selects the driving ranges required. Six positions are marked on the quadrant, P, R, N, 3, 2 and 1 which indicate the following operating conditions.

P—Parking:

The gearbox is in the neutral position. The engine may be started and run without any drive being transmitted to the rear wheels. A mechanical device locks the transmission and prevents the car from moving in either direction. This must never be selected when the car is in motion.

R—Reverse:

As its name implies is for driving backwards. This position should not be selected while the car is travelling forwards.

N—Neutral:

The gearbox is in the neutral position as in P but the transmission is not locked.

3—Automatic:

When selected from rest the car pulls away in 1st speed and changes automatically into 2nd and 3rd at speeds dependent upon the accelerator pedal position and the speed of the car. Down changes are similarly effected.

2—Locking in second:

This position gives automatic changes as in 3 but never moves into 3 or high gear. If 2 is selected when in high

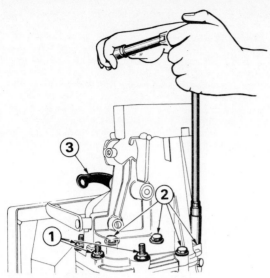

FIG 6:36 Fitting the rear housing

Key to Fig.6:36 1 Three double thread studs 2 Four securing bolts 3 Selector lever

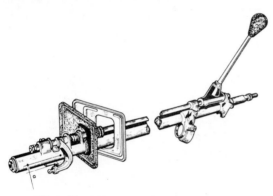

FIG 6:37 Adjusting the gear change lever

gear in 3 range the down change will be made only when the speed of the car is less than 68 mile/hr (110 km/h).

1—Locking in first:

In this position the transmission is locked in first (low or bottom) gear. When selected from either 2 or 3 range the change will be made only when the car speed is below 41 mile/hr (66 km/h).

These two latter ranges are most useful for good performance on long hill climbs or when descending to give engine braking.

In addition to the selection options mentioned above it is possible to obtain down changes by the use of the accelerator pedal alone. The pedal may be depressed beyond the full throttle position to what is called the 'kick-down' position. Moving the pedal down to this position will cause an immediate change down to a lower ratio or increase the road speed at which the change in the selected gear ratio is effected.

Towing:

In the event of a tow being required after an accident or some mechanical failure, the selector lever should be set to N and a speed of 30 mile/hr (50 km/h) be observed *provided that* the transmission is not damaged.

If a faster tow or a journey of more than about 30 miles is necessary the car should be towed on its front wheels.

Note that it is not possible to start the engine by towing or pushing the car.

It may be of assistance in assessing the performance of the transmission if the normal gearchange speeds are given:

Throttle position	1–2	2–3	3–2	2–1
Light	8	16	14	6 mile/hr
¾	11	23	18	8 mile/hr
Full	23	57	37	19 mile/hr
Kick-down	35	60	59	32 mile/hr

6:9 Maintenance

No maintenance is required on the automatic transmission other than keeping the oil level at the correct height and seeing that any accumulation of mud on the casing or ventilation holes is removed as this will seriously affect the cooling of the unit.

To check the oil level the car must be standing on level ground and the transmission at normal working temperature. Apply the handbrake and allow the engine to idle with N selected. The level on the dipstick should be between the upper MAXI and lower MINI, reference marks, noting that the difference between the two marks is equivalent to about 1 pint (.6 litre). The fluids recom-

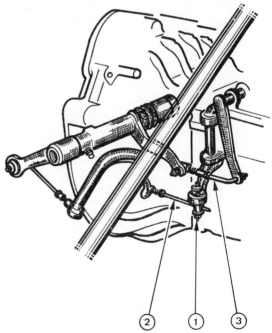

FIG 6:38 Adjusting the gearbox selector controls

Key to Fig 6:38 1 Pin nut 2 Selector rod 3 Selector lever

mended by the manufacturer are Esso A.AQ.AFT.2974A or DEXRON B 10696 and the total capacity is 9.1 pints (5.2 litres).

At the intervals laid down in the Owners Hand Book the transmission should be drained by removing the drain plug on the rear face of the oil pan. This is preferably done when warm, but care must be taken as the fluid may be at a very high temperature and injury may be caused if allowed to contact the hands.

Refilling is best carried out by first pouring in $3\frac{1}{2}$ pints (2 litres) of fluid, then start the engine and allow it to idle while sufficient fluid is added to bring it up to the MAXI mark on the dipstick.

The manufacturers advise against any adjustments of the transmission or its controls and in the event of a breakdown the car should be taken to an accredited agent for attention or a new unit fitted. For those owners who feel able to carry out this operation for themselves, instructions on the removal of the transmission are given.

Removing the transmission:

Disconnect the exhaust pipe and the speedometer drive.

Unbolt the propeller shaft at the back of the transmission and move the rear axle rearwards as for the removal of the manual gearbox.

Disconnect the linkage between the selector lever and the operating lever on the transmission.

Disconnect the leads to the inhibitor switch, noting carefully their positions for later reassembly.

Take the weight of the engine on a suitable garage jack and remove the bolts securing the engine to the transmission. Remove the oil filler pipe and cover the hole to prevent the entry of any foreign matter.

Remove the protecting plate under the converter, then undo the securing screws from the converter plate. This may be done through the hole in the flywheel by turning the crankshaft a little at a time. Remove the crossmember behind the transmission.

Move the engine on its jack as far forwards as the flexible mountings will allow and then pull out the transmission unit towards the rear. Make sure that the converter assembly remains with the transmission and does not move forwards with the engine during this operation.

Refitting:

This is a reversal of the removal procedure but be particularly careful of the two centring tubes on the front face of the converter housing.

6:10 Gear change controls

The steering column gear change lever assembly is shown in **FIG 6:37** and if it is to be overhauled it will be necessary first to remove the steering column. Be sure to mark the position of the lower, C shaped, lever on the splines of the control rod, as incorrect angular refitting will seriously affect its operation.

The dimension a is important and is determined as follows:

On early cars the centre to centre distance on the C shaped lower lever is 95 mm and on later cars it is 80 mm. Dimension a on the early type must be 18 ± 2 mm and on the later type it is 22 ± 2 mm.

The selector controls on the gearbox are shown in **FIG 6:38** and may or may not have a locking device in the neutral position. To adjust the first type:

Place the steering column selector lever in 2nd gear and then slacken the pin nut 1.

Mark the maximum play positions permitted by the selector lever and then place the selector lever in the middle position and tighten selector rod 2 by tightening the pin nut 1.

Check the movement in all gears.

To adjust the mechanism with the neutral locking device proceed as follows:

Place the gear selector lever in neutral and slacken the pin nut 1.

Ensure that the selector lever 3 is in the neutral ball lock position and adjust as before.

6:11 Fault diagnosis (manual gearbox)

(a) Jumping out of gear

1 Misalignment between transmission and clutch housing
2 Worn shift detent parts
3 Worn clutch shaft bearing
4 Worn teeth of dog clutch
5 Improper adjustment of linkage
6 Worn main shaft bearings
7 Worn countershaft thrust washers
8 Excessive main shaft end play
9 Worn counter gear or counter gear bearings

(b) Noisy gearbox

1 Insufficient lubrication
2 Worn or damaged bearings
3 Excessive end play in main shaft
4 Worn or damaged gear teeth
5 Speedometer gears worn or damaged

(c) Difficulty in engaging gears

1 Incorrect clutch pedal adjustment
2 Worn synchromesh cones

(d) Oil leaks

1 Damaged joint washers
2 Worn or damaged oil seals
3 Transmission covers loose or faces damaged.

NOTES

CHAPTER 7

PROPELLER SHAFT, REAR AXLE,
REAR SUSPENSION

7:1 The drive shaft

The drive shaft consists of a torque tube and propeller shaft which has its thrust and centre torque locations almost at the centre of gravity of the vehicle. The shaft is supported at the front end by a needle bearing and at its centre section by an intermediate bearing. The centre bearing is installed with rubber bushes to dampen out vibrations.

The only routine maintenance required is to lubricate the torque tube ball joint and the centre bearing at 1800 mile intervals with multi-purpose grease.

7:2 Removing and replacing the centre needle bearing

In order to remove the centre bearing it is necessary to use the special tool Part number 8.042Z which comprises a threaded rod, a sheet metal spacer, a split washer which seats on the spacer and a wrench. To remove the bearing proceed as follows:

1 Hold the torque tube in a vice and remove the centre bearing lubricating nipple.
2 Lubricate the inside of the torque tube abundantly with oil to facilitate the removal of the bearing and cage.

3 Engage the puller threaded portion so that the finger lies in a horizontal position (see 2 in **FIG 7:1**). Push the puller through the rear end of the tube.
4 When the head of the puller has reached its position past the bearing, rotate the puller over half a turn, so that the finger assumes a vertical position.
5 Refer to **FIG 7:2** and fit the sheet metal spacer C, on the torque tube by means of two nuts. Position the backing washer B, and install the nut.
6 The bearing can now be withdrawn by tightening the nut.

Replacing the centre needle bearing:

To replace a centre needle bearing it is again necessary to use the special tool 8.043Z, which comprises an impact pusher and a spacer. Fit the bearing as follows:

1 With the torque tube held in a vice, lubricate with an abundant quantity of oil to facilitate the installation of the centre bearing and cage.
2 Dip the centre bearing and cage in engine oil, engage them inside the torque tube while tapping the cage with the handle of a hammer.

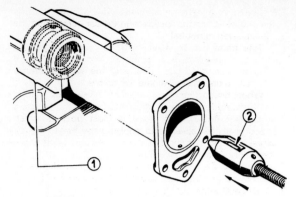

FIG 7:1 Engaging puller in centre bearing

Key to Fig 7:1   1 Centre bearing cage   2 Puller finger

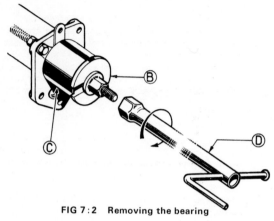

FIG 7:2 Removing the bearing

Key to Fig 7:2   **B** Backing washer   **C** Sheet metal spacer   **D** Wrench

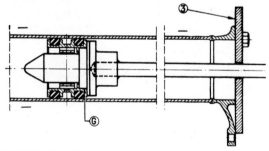

FIG 7:3 Position of spacer when refitting bearing

Key to Fig 7:3   3 Plate bolted to torque tube   **G** Spacer

3 Install the bearing and cage in position using the impact pusher as follows:

Engage the pusher head with the spacer G (see **FIG 7:3**), inside the bearing and bolt plate 3 to the torque tube. Using the special tool 5 (see **FIG 7:4**), engage the bearing cage until the washer 4, rests on the plate 3. The bearing is now in position and the impact pusher can be removed.

7:3 The rear axle

A cutaway view of the rear axle fitted to most models can be seen in **FIG 7:5**. It is unusual in having a steel worm driving a bronze wheel.

The advantages of this system include a lower centre of gravity and a lower floor profile, giving more room inside for the passengers. In theory it has the disadvantage of being noisy with more friction but these drawbacks have been largely nullified by the manufacturers.

The rear axle oil level should be checked at every 1800 miles and drained and refilled at every 3600 miles. In no case should the rear axle special lubricant, Essolube VT or Esso gear oil GP.90, be mixed with another lubricant. In case of doubt arising about the type of oil used, carefully drain and flush out the rear axle before refilling.

Some estate cars and some later saloons have a more conventional hypoid bevel gear rear axle.

7:4 Removing the rear axle

1 Disconnect the rear shock absorbers from the vehicle floor.
2 Disconnect the stabilizer bar on the bodywork, right-hand side.
3 Disconnect the brake control sheaths from the vehicle floor, also the anti-roll bar if fitted.
4 Disconnect the brake hydraulic hose.
5 Disconnect the brake control cables from the equalizer.
6 Lift the vehicle from the rear end to remove the helical springs.
7 Remove the exhaust pipe clamping collar from the exhaust manifold and from the clutch housing.
8 Fit the engine support stirrup into position, as follows: Below the engine flywheel case when removing the axle only; below the engine crankcase lower sump when removal of the gearbox is required.
9 Disconnect the change speed and clutch control assembly.
10 Remove the brake equalizer support plate.
11 Remove the engine rear support crossmember by undoing the two nuts on the underside of the floor and 1 screw on the tunnel inside the vehicle.
12 Operate the stirrup screw to lower the assembly approximately 70 mm.
13 Remove the torque tube ball joint cover and support attachment bolts.
14 Separate the axle from the universal joint.
15 Lift the vehicle body from the rear a sufficient height to allow the removal of the axle and wheel assembly.

To refit the rear axle reverse the removal operations but first ensure that the rear engine support is clean and clear of oil, grease or paint which could affect its useful life. Smear both mating surfaces with a sealing paste. When reinstalling the rear springs orientate the nose of the lower first coil to the rear.

Bleed the brakes.

7:5 Removing and replacing the rear axle shaft

1 Jack the car at the rear, remove the three wheel attaching nuts and remove the wheel.
2 Remove the countersunk screws and remove the brake drum.
3 Disconnect the bearing retaining flanges from the rear axle tube.

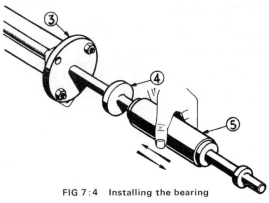

FIG 7:4   Installing the bearing

Key to Fig 7:4   3 Plate   4 Washer   5 Impact installer

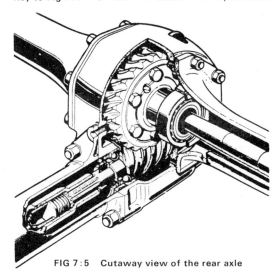

FIG 7:5   Cutaway view of the rear axle

4 Remove the wheel shaft, using a suitable puller fixed to the three wheel attachment studs (see **FIG 7:6**).

Before reinstalling the shaft, smear the bearing faces of the flange and axle tube with sealing paste. With the shaft in position, tighten the nuts of the flange to a torque of 7.23 to 10.8 lb ft.

7:6 Diagnosing rear axle faults

Due to the special tooling and gauging required for the reassembly of the rear axle it is not advised that the assembly should be stripped. Much can be learned by observing symptoms during the operation of the car. The most common rear axle complaint is noise. Care must be taken to ensure that the noise is not caused by the engine, transmission, tyres, wheel bearings or some other part of the car.

Before road testing the car ensure that there is sufficient lubricant in the axle housing and inflate the tyres to the correct pressures. Drive the car far enough to warm the lubricant to its normal operating temperature before making the tests.

Engine or exhaust noise can be detected by running the engine at various speeds with the car parked and the transmission in neutral.

Tyre noise can be detected by running the car over various road surfaces. Tyre noise is minimized on a smooth asphalt surface. Changing the wheels around can help to detect or eliminate tyre noises.

Wheel bearing noise can often be detected by jacking up the car and feeling for roughness when the wheel is rotated. Wheel bearing noise is most obvious when coasting at low speed, and applying the brakes lightly while the car is moving will often reduce or eliminate the noise of a defective bearing.

When all the above conditions have been eliminated test the car for axle noise under the following conditions:

1 Drive: Gradual acceleration on a level road.
2 Cruise: Constant speed operation at normal road speed.
3 Float: Use only enough throttle to keep the car from driving the engine.
4 Coast: Throttle closed with engine braking the car.

Backlash or play in the running gear can be checked by driving the car on a smooth road at 25 mile/hr and lightly pressing and releasing the accelerator pedal. Backlash is indicated by a slapping noise with each movement of the accelerator pedal. Raising the car on a ramp will enable a more detailed examination to be made.

7:7 Rear suspension

The rear suspension comprises coil springs and telescopic shock absorbers. The coil springs are mounted directly on the axle tube and are inclined slightly to the

FIG 7:6   Removing the rear axle shaft

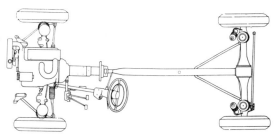

FIG 7:7   Plan view showing suspension arrangement

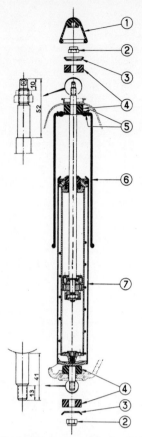

FIG 7:8   Exploded view of rear shock absorber

Key to Fig 7:8   1 Cap   2 Nylstop nut   3 Cup washer
4 Rubber thrust washer   5 Upper sleeve mounting
6 Upper sleeve   7 Shock absorber body

front. The shock absorbers are fitted just ahead of the
coil springs and are again inclined slightly to the front.
Radius arms are fitted to absorb the reactions of braking
and acceleration. The arrangement of the suspension can
be seen in **FIG 7:7.**

A stabilizer bar ensures lateral connection between
the rear axle and the body. Its length, as well as its
attachment points, is designed with a view to eliminating
all lateral reactions of the vehicle.

7:8 Rear shock absorber removal and refitting

The rear shock absorbers are of the hydraulic telescopic damper type and are sealed units requiring no maintenance. No dismantling is possible so units must be
changed when no longer serviceable.

Removal:

1 An exploded view of the rear shock absorber is shown
   in **FIG 7:8.** From the rear floor of the car remove the
   cap 1.
2 Unscrew the nylstop nut 2, holding the rod through
   the flat portion at the end.
3 Remove the cup 3, and the rubber thrust washer 4.
4 From the rear axle tube unscrew the nylstop nut 2.

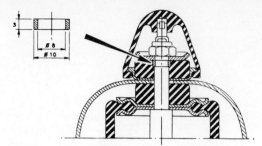

FIG 7:9   Shock absorber upper attachment—early
models

5 Remove the cup 3 and rubber thrust washer 4.
6 Compress the shock absorber and remove from the
   car.

Refitting:

From car No. 404 4.050.013 to 404.067.885 a 3 mm
spacer was installed as part of the upper attachment to
eliminate knocking (see **FIG 7:9**). From car No. 404
4.067.885 the shock absorber rod was made 3 mm
longer in order to eliminate the spacer.

1 Place the thrust washers 4, on the top and bottom of
   the shock absorber rod.
2 On the rear floor of the car, with the shock absorber
   held in position, seat the thrust washer and the cup 3.
3 Screw on a new nylstop nut and torque load to 12.6
   to 18 lb ft.
4 On the rear axle tube, extend the shock absorber so
   that the top comes against the support.
5 Install the thrust washer, cup and a new nylstop nut
   and torque load to 12.6 to 18 lb ft.
6 Check that the rod protrudes 9.5 to 10 mm at the top
   attachment (see **FIG 7:8**). Install the cap 1.

7:9 Fault diagnosis

(a) Noisy axle

1 Insufficient or incorrect lubricant
2 Worn bearings
3 Worn gears

(b) Excessive backlash

1 Worn gears, bearings or bearing housings
2 Worn axle shaft splines
3 Worn universal joints
4 Loose or broken wheel studs

(c) Oil leakage

1 Defective seals in hub
2 Defective shaft seal

(d) Vibration

1 Propeller shaft out of alignment
2 Worn universal joint bearings

(e) Rattles

1 Rubber bushes in damper attachments worn
2 Dampers loose

(f) Settling

1 Weak or broken springs

CHAPTER 8

FRONT SUSPENSION AND HUBS

8:1 Description of system

The suspension units on each side consist of a telescopic shock absorber and a coil spring, resting on lower wishbones. The coils are mounted above the shock absorbers putting them above the level of the wheels as can be seen in the sectioned view of the suspension in **FIG 8:1**. This factor allows large wheel movements on bounce and rebound which evens out even the roughest of roads. Radius arms run from the lower location points of the spring legs forward to the chassis where they are rubber bushed. These take braking reactions and complete the suspension system.

Toe-in is the only front end angle that is adjustable. It is necessary to renew bent parts to re-establish the correct angles in the event of any misalignment.

The wheels and drums are balanced both statically and dynamically at the factory and must be marked before disassembly so that they can be replaced in their correct positions.

8:2 Routine maintenance

At every 1800 miles lubricate the grease nipple on the lower swivel and stub axle assembly. Before injecting grease clean and examine the nipples for damage and if necessary renew the nipples.

At every 10,000 miles, remove the hub cap, clean out all the old grease and repack the cap with multi-purpose grease.

8:3 Front hub removal and dismantling

1 Jack up the front of the car and remove the front wheel and brake drum after marking their relative position.
2 Remove the hub grease cap, unlock and remove the stub axle nut.
3 Remove the flat D washer and withdraw the inner cone and race of the outer hub bearing (see **FIG 8:2**).
4 Remove the hub together with the outer cup and race of the inner hub bearing and the grease retainer. The inner cone of the inner bearing will stay on the stub axle.
5 From the hub, drift out the outer cup of the outer bearing and the outer cup and race of the inner bearing together with the grease retainer.

Thoroughly clean all parts. Bearings that have been in service must be cleaned before they are inspected. Wash the bearings in clean flushing oil or white spirit and blow out with compressed air. Examine the bearings for corrosion and for discoloration resulting from overheating. A light brown discoloration may be due to

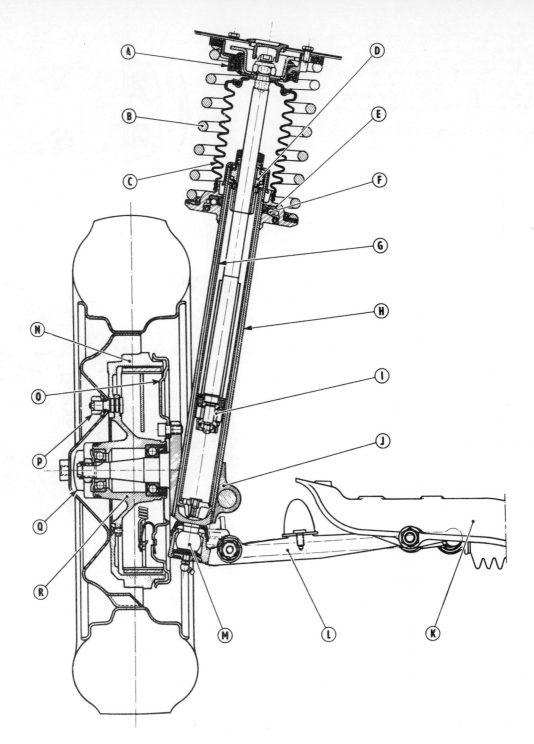

FIG 8:1 Sectioned view through the front suspension

Key to Fig 8:1   A Shock absorber upper mount   B Coil spring   C Rubber bellows   D Shock absorber cover nut   E Coil spring lower seat   F Ballbearing   G Shock absorber body   H Shock absorber housing   I Piston   J Spindle assembly   K Front crossmember   L Lower arms assembly   M Lower arms ball joint   N Brake drum   O Brake backing plate   P Wheel lug nut (45 lb ft)   Q Wheel bearing grease cap   R Hub

lubricant stain and is not detrimental. When rotating the bearings to check for wear or damage apply axial pressure to bring the balls firmly into contact with the races. Cleanliness is essential during inspection and replacement to avoid contamination with any abrasive substance, otherwise the highly polished mating surfaces will be damaged, thus increasing the rate of wear.

8:4 Front hub reassembly and refitting

1 Grease the hub and the bearings with multi-purpose grease.
2 Drift the outer cup of the outer bearing into position in the hub (see **FIG 8:2**).
3 Drift the outer cup of the inner bearing into the hub and note the position of both cups when installed (see **FIG 8:2**).
4 Liberally grease the race of the inner bearing, insert the cup of the inner bearing, and drift the grease retainer into position with its lip facing towards the inside of the hub.
5 Place the cone of the inner bearing on the stub axle in position against the inner shoulder.
6 Install the hub on the stub axle, grease and install the outer bearing race and the flat D washer.
7 Hold the D washer against the bearing cone, install and tighten the stub axle nut to a torque of 21.6 lb ft. Release the nut and re-tighten to 7.2 lb ft. Lock the nut with a new splitpin.
8 Install the hub cap smeared with grease.
9 Install the brake drum and wheels, ensuring that the marks made when dismantling are aligned, torque the wheel nuts to 45 lb ft and lower the car to the ground.

8:5 Front suspension unit removal

1 Jack up the front of the car and place stands under the crossmember.
2 Remove the wheel, the hub (see **Section 8:3**), the brake drum and the brake backing plate.
3 Disconnect the steering connecting link at the steering arm.
4 Unlock and remove the front arm to side rail yoke attaching shaft.
5 Remove the three upper screws attaching the suspension unit to the wing valance (see **FIG 8:3**).
6 Remove the assembly complete and recover the rubber washer of the front arm from the car.

8:6 Front suspension unit dismantling

1 With the suspension unit removed from the car mount it in a vice.
2 Unlock and remove the rod stop nut at the top of the shock absorber assembly.
3 Remove from the shock absorber unit the following items: safety cup, upper support, coil spring, spring lower backing cup with rubber protector and the shock absorber upper protector cup.
4 Remove the ball cage from the pivot body, and the shock absorber body castellated nut.
5 Withdraw the piston rod slowly to avoid oil splashing and remove the piston rod assembly together with the ringed bearing and bearing spacer. When the shock absorber body is replaced, renew the nylon spacer and thrust bearing seal.

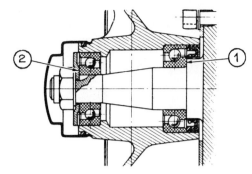

FIG 8:2 Front hub bearings and grease retainer assembly

Key to Fig 8:2   1 Outer hub bearing   2 Inner hub bearing

FIG 8:3 Upper suspension fixing screws on valance

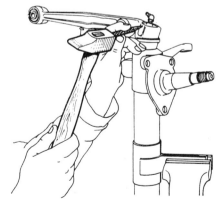

FIG 8:4 Removing the ball head snap ring

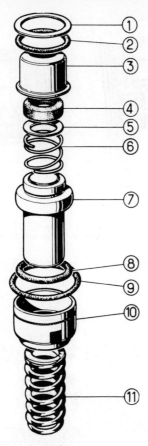

FIG 8:5 The upper suspension seal assembly

Key to Fig 8:5 1 Backing washer 2 O-ring 3 Upper cup 4 Rod seal 5 Recessed washer 6 Rod seal spring 7 Rod guide 8 Guide seal 9 Spacer seal 10 Bearing spacer 11 Spring

6 Remove the assembly from the vice ˙and turn upside down to drain the oil.

7 When draining is complete, remove the valve support and cylinder assembly from the shock absorber body.

8 Replace the assembly in a vice with the lower arm on top to permit removal of the ballhead.

9 Using a sharp punch and working through the hole provided for this purpose, drive out the ball head cap snap ring (see **FIG 8:4**). Complete the operation with a screwdriver used as a lever. Remove the cap and the Belleville washers used to hold the nylon half bearing shells.

10 Unlock and remove the ball head castellated nut.

11 Using a mallet, drive the arm assembly upwards to remove the ball head from its taper. The ball head will remain in the arm between the two half bearing shells.

12 Remove the ball head rubber oil seal.

13 Remove the front arm from the rear arm, noting the order of assembly of the following parts: rear backing cup, rear half cone, front half cone, front backing cup, front arm and backing washer.

8:7 Front suspension unit reassembly

When reassembling the unit inspect and renew parts as necessary. It is permissible to use the original shock absorber body and steering swivel with a new shock absorber mechanism or to use the original mechanism with a new body and swivel.

Install the nylon spacer with the chamfered edge uppermost, and the thrust bearing seal onto the shock absorber body. Inspect the shock absorber rod and ensure that it is not bent.

Carefully avoid buckling of the spacer seal (see **FIG 8:5**), item 9 as this would result in leakage. Check for the correct positioning of the rod seal 4, during reassembly. A circular bead is formed in the seal to facilitate the matching recessed washer 5. The cambered side of the the washer is mounted against the rod seal spring 6.

1 Clean out the inside of the shock absorber body, inspect and renew parts where necessary.

2 Install the special spacer F (see **FIG 8:6**), on the rod of the rod-piston-and-bearing assembly and compress the rod seal spring by tightening the nyloc nut until the cup 3, of the rod seal is tight on the bearing. This is necessary to avoid distortion of the backing washer 1, when tightening the castellated nut, which would result in damage to the rubber O-ring.

3 Carefully clean the cylinder, support and valve sub-assembly and install it in the shock absorber body.

4 Fill the shock absorber with 350 cc of **Esso Oleofluid 40.EP.**

5 Engage the assembly into the cylinder and push down slowly until the bearing spacer 10 (see **FIG 8:5**), is correctly positioned on top of the cylinder and shock absorber body. The spacer should be 3 to 3.5 mm (.118 to .138 inch) above the threaded body. On 404 models prior to 4.016.997 this figure should not

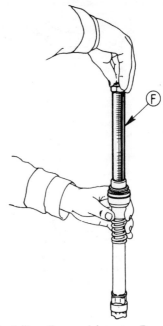

FIG 8:6 Installing the special spacer F on the shock absorber rod during assembly

exceed 20 to 25 mm (.079 to .099 inch). This is due to a modification of the castellated nut.

6 Install and tighten the castellated nut to a torque of 44 to 50 lb ft.

7 Remove the nyloc nut and special spacer F from the shock absorber rod. Work the rod in and out to check for free sliding and rotation movement, leaving the rod in the extended position.

8 Re-install the pivot bearing ball cage and lubricate with multi-purpose grease.

9 Insert the upper attachment cup (item 1 of **FIG 8:7**), into the rubber protector using a small quantity of cement to stick the cup inside the protector so that it will remain in position during assembly.

10 Secure the rubber protector to the spring lower backing cup with a clamp and position the coil spring on the backing cup (see **FIG 8:8**).

11 Place the shock absorber upper support on top of the spring and position the safety cup in the upper support by means of the tab and groove (see **FIG 8:7**).

12 Compress the spring assembly with a spring compressor and centre in position on top of the shock absorber. Position the rubber protector upper cup (see item 2, **FIG 8:7**), and as the lower cup comes to rest on the thrust bearing, the shock absorber rod will appear in the safety cup, if the rod has been maintained in its extended position. Failure of the rod to appear in the safety cup will mean that the rod has been accidentally pushed down and the assembly will have to be removed and re-installed with the rod fully extended.

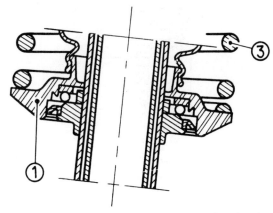

FIG 8:8 The coil spring lower thrust bearing showing modified type from which the spring backing rubber has been deleted

Key to Fig 8:8   1 Spring backing cup   3 Coil spring

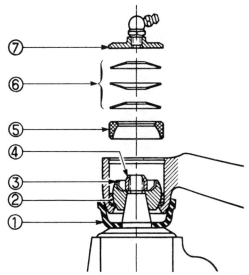

FIG 8:9   The lower suspension ball head joint

Key to Fig 8:9   1 Rubber seal   2 Upper half bearing shell   3 Ball head   4 Ball head nut   5 Lower half bearing shell   6 Belleville washer   7 Ball head cap

FIG 8:7   The coil spring prepared for installation

Key to Fig 8:7   1 Upper attachment cup   2 Rubber protector

13 Fit a new nyloc nut to the shock absorber rod, tighten to a torque of 35 to 43 lb ft and remove the spring compressor.

14 On the other end of the suspension unit, install on the ball head in following order: rubber seal (item 1 of **FIG 8:9**), rear wishbone arm, upper half of bearing shell and the ball head 3. Note that the upper half of the bearing shell 2, is the narrower of the two half shells.

15 Install a new castellated nut, tighten to a torque of 30 to 36 lb ft and lock by staking the two milled sections of the nut provided for this purpose.

16 Install in the following order: lower half of bearing 5, the three Belleville washers 6, and the ball head cap.

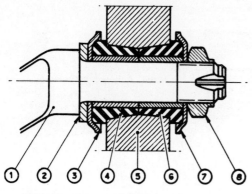

FIG 8:10 Front arm attachment to rear arm

Key to Fig 8:10   1 Front arm   2 Backing washer
3 Backing cup   4 Half cone bush   5 Rear arm   6 Half
cone bush   7 Rear cup washer   8 Retaining nut

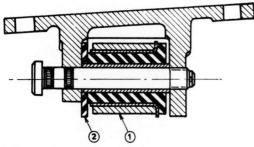

**FIG 8:11 Front arm attachment on the crossmember
yoke**

Key to Fig 8:11   1 Front arm bush eye   2 Rubber
spacing washer

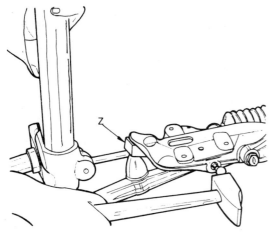

**FIG 8:12 Driving in the serrated pins with block Z in
position**

Note particularly the correct position of the Belleville
washers.

17 Compress the assembly and fit a new circlip, ensuring
that it seats correctly in its groove.

18 Fit the front arm to the rear arm of the wishbone by
assembling the parts as shown in **FIG 8:10,** leaving
the nut finger tight for final tightening on installation
in the car. Lubricate the ball head joint with multi-
purpose grease.

8:8 Refitting the front suspension unit

1 Place the suspension unit under the wing valance,
supporting it under the lower ball head. Ensure that
the drain hole in the safety cup is positioned to the
inside of the car.

2 Fit the three upper support screws and tighten them
to a torque of 9 to 10.8 lb ft. Fit the special plug to the
centre hole in the wing valance.

3 Install the wishbone rear arm in the crossmember side
rail yoke and the front arm to the crossmember yoke
with the rubber washer between the rubber bushing
and the front part of the yoke as shown in **FIG 8:11.**
Insert both retaining pins from the front and drive in
up to the serrated portions of the pins.

4 Install the brake backing plate with the grease catcher
cup between the backing plate and stub axle.

5 Check that the protruding part of the upper brake
plate attaching screw does not foul the shock
absorber body, tighten the screws to a torque of
39.8 to 47 lb ft and lock by centre punching the
protruding portion of the screws.

6 Place a bead of plastic sealing compound around
the junction of the brake backing plate and the stub
axle flange.

7 Install the hub and brake drum and tighten the stub
axle nut to 21.7 lb ft, loosen the nut and finally tighten
to 6.2 lb ft and lock with a new splitpin.

8 Fit the hub cap and install the road wheel.

9 Lower the front of the car to the ground and place a
21 mm (.867 inch) block between the rebound rubber
and the crossmember (see **FIG 8:12**). Load the front
of the car until the block is held between the rubber
and the crossmember. The rubber bushes are now in
a static position.

10 Drive in both rubber bush attaching pins (see
Operation 3), fit and tighten the nuts to a torque of
57.8 to 65 lb ft and lock with new splitpins.

11 Tighten the front arm to rear arm attaching nut to a
torque of 21.7 to 28.9 lb ft.

12 Install the steering arm and connecting link and
tighten the nut to a torque of 36.7 to 39.7 lb ft.

13 Bleed and adjust the brakes, if necessary. Check and
adjust the toe-in.

8:9 Front crossmember removal and refitting

1 Disconnect the battery and support the front of the
engine from above with a cross bar and adjustable
hook attached to the eyelet on the cylinder block
beneath the coil.

2 Raise the front of the car and support it on stands
placed beneath the body lower front crossmember.

3 Remove the screws attaching the engine front
mountings to the front suspension crossmember and
raise the engine slightly.

4 Remove the screws attaching the steering gear housing to the front crossmember.

5 Remove the nuts and serrated bolts from the wishbone rubber bush attachments to the crossmember brackets and lower the wishbone arms.

6 Remove the brake pipe attachment screws at the front crossmember.

7 Remove the six screws attaching the crossmember to the side rails and withdraw the front crossmember from the car.

Refitting:

Refitting is the reverse procedure but note the following points:

1 When fitting the rear wishbone arms to the crossmember brackets, drive the serrated pins in from the front, up to the serrations only.

2 Lower the front of the car and fit a 31 mm thick block between the rebound rubber and the crossmember.

3 Load the front of the car until the block is held firmly.

4 Drive the serrated pins fully home, tighten and lock the retaining nuts.

5 Reconnect the battery and check the front wheel alignment.

8:10 Suspension geometry

The castor and camber angles, the kingpin inclination and the wheel alignment of the front suspension are design settings that have a very important effect on the handling of the car. With the exception of the front wheel toe-in, all the settings are determined during manufacture and no adjustment is provided.

The dimensions for checking the geometry are given in Technical Data, but the use of specialized equipment is essential for accurate results and it is suggested that these checks be left to a fully equipped Service Station.

8:11 Wheel balancing

The need for wheel balancing has become increasingly pronounced with the use of independent suspension and the light steering efforts designed into modern cars.

Wheel shimmy (a light tremor noticeable at the steering wheel), or wheel wobble (a pronounced tremor noticeable at the steering wheel, caused by a self-sustained movement of the road wheels to the left and right when moving forward), can both be due to wheel and tyre out of balance. Although in some cases repositioning the wheel relative to the hub may effect a cure, the only accurate method to correct an out of balance force is to use suitable wheel balancing equipment.

8:12 Fault diagnosis

(a) Wheel wobble

1 Worn hub bearings
2 Broken or weak front springs
3 Uneven tyre wear
4 Worn suspension linkage
5 Loose wheel fixings

(b) 'Bottoming' of suspension

1 Check 2 in (a)
2 Rebound rubbers worn or missing
3 Dampers (shock absorbers) not working

(c) Heavy steering

1 Neglected swivel pin lubrication
2 Wrong suspension geometry

(d) Excessive tyre wear

1 Check 4 in (a), 3 in (b) and 2 in (c)

(e) Rattles

1 Check 2 in (a)
2 Lubrication neglected, rubber bushes worn
3 Damper mountings loose
4 Wishbone mountings loose or worn

(f) Excessive rolling

1 Check 2 in (a) and 3 in (b)

NOTES

CHAPTER 9

THE STEERING GEAR

9:1 Description

The rack and pinion type steering gear incorporates an automatic play take-up device consisting of two spring-loaded plungers pressing the rack on the pinion.

The plunger located on the pinion side takes up the steering wheel angular play, while the one on the rack side acts as a steering damper and takes up axial play.

The assembly (see **FIG 9:1**), which is of simple design and high strength, consists of an aluminium sleeve or housing, inside which the rack slides under the action of a helical tooth pinion integral with the steering wheel shaft.

The rack is connected to the steering levers through two adjustable connecting links, each fitted with two end fittings. On the lefthand side the connection is through a ball head fitting housed within the rack and on the righthand side through an eye end fitting screwed into the rack.

The ball head permits accurate parallelism adjustment, one full turn of the ball head is equal to 3 mm toe-in or flare according to the direction of rotation.

The gearing down of the steering mechanism is 1:18.6 corresponding to 3.75 full steering wheel turns between stops.

9:2 Routine maintenance

The steering assembly has eight lubrication points which need attention every 1800 miles. The steering gear housing should only be lightly lubricated while all the other points should have normal grease gun service using multi-purpose grease.

The grease nipples are as follows:

Left- and righthand kingpins.
Left- and righthand steering lever ball heads.
Steering gear housing.
Rack tappets and ball heads

9:3 Removing the rack and pinion unit

1 Place the car on a ramp or over a pit with the front wheels in the straight-ahead position.
2 Disconnect the battery.
3 Remove the upper yoke bolt to disconnect the steering column from the flexible joint. The steering assembly as fitted to the car can be seen in **FIG 9:2**.
4 Disconnect the steering gear connecting links from the steering arms.
5 Unscrew the two steering gear housing attachment screws.
6 Remove the assembly from the car.

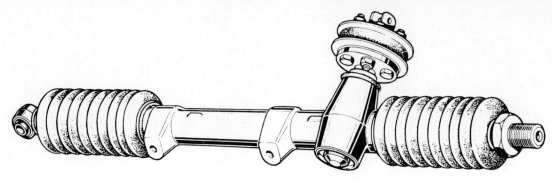

FIG 9:1   The rack and pinion assembly

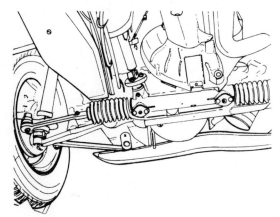

FIG 9:2   View of front axle and steering gear

FIG 9:3   Exploded view of the pinion assembly

AWAY FROM PINION	PINION SIDE

FIG 9:4   The rack dampers

Key to Fig 9:4   1 Flange   2 Adjusting shims   3 Nylon spacer

9:4 Dismantling the rack and pinion

1 Remove the eyebolt from the inner end of the right-hand side connecting link.
2 Remove the rubber boot clamps at the connecting links.
3 Release the locknut and remove the rack eye from the righthand end of the steering rack.
4 Release the ball head locknut and remove the left-hand connecting link.
5 Remove the rubber boots and the rack housing cap.
6 Unlock and remove the pinion nut. An exploded view of the pinion assembly can be seen in **FIG 9:3**.
7 Remove the flange screws and take out the rack damper plungers, springs and, on the pinion end, the spacer and shims (see **FIG 9:4**). The shims on the pinion side should be retained for reassembly. Withdraw the pinion, followed by the rack, from the housing.
8 Remove the circlip and the pinion lower ballbearing from the rack housing.
9 Remove the flexible rubber coupling and the rubber O-ring from the pinion.
10 Hold the rack in a vice with protected jaws and unscrew the ball head housing.
11 Remove the ball head, adjusting shim, shell and backing spring or Belleville washers. Belleville washers replaced the backing spring as from car No. 4.019.543.

9:5 Reassembling the rack and pinion

1 Place the rack vertically in a vice with protected jaws.
2 Determine the thickness of the ball head housing adjusting shims as described in **Section 9:6**.
3 Check the depth of recess X in the end of the steering rack (see **FIG 9:5**).
4 On models up to 4.019.542 the depth of this recess was 22.5 mm (.885 inch). On models after that serial number the depth of the recess was increased to 23 mm (.905 inch). If the depth of the recess is 23 mm (.905 inch), install a .5 mm (.020 inch) shim in the bottom of the recess. It is most important that the shim is only fitted in a recess with the greater depth.
5 With the shim fitted, install the 13 Belleville washers as shown in **FIG 9:6**.
6 Install the ball head and shell, which is centred by the special pin No. 8.0703D, and the shim on the end of the rack as determined in **Section 9:6**.

7 Screw on a new ball head housing, tighten to a torque of 30 to 46 lb ft and lock by staking.

8 Install the pinion ballbearing in the rack housing and fit the retaining clip.

9 Fit the flexible coupling to the pinion, tighten and lock the bolts.

10 Insert the rack in the housing and position it so that the end opposite the ball head protrudes by 98 mm (3.846 inches) as shown in **FIG 9 : 7**.

11 Install the pinion, fitted with a new O-ring seal so that the yoke holes are aligned as shown in **FIG 9 : 7**. Fit a new pinion nut, tighten to a torque of 11 to 14 lb ft and lock by staking. Fit the housing cap.

12 Refer to **Section 9 : 7** and determine the thickness of the shims to be inserted between the damper flange and the thrust spacer of the damper, at the pinion end of the rack.

13 Install the rack dampers and tighten the flange screws to a torque of 7.25 to 9 lb ft.

14 Check for stiffness by operating the rack in both directions and fit the rubber boots.

15 Screw the lefthand connecting link and locknut onto the rack ball shank so that a 24 mm (.945 inch) dimension exists between the ball head housing and the locknut, with the connecting link aligned with the rack centre line (see **FIG 9 : 8**). Tighten the locknut finger tight.

16 Screw the rack eye into the righthand of the rack so that the threaded portion protrudes by 9.5 to 11 mm (.374 to .433 inch), with the locknut against the rack end face (see **FIG 9 : 9**).

Note that the eyebolt and locknuts are left finger tight for adjustment of the wheel alignment after the assembly has been installed in the car.

9 : 6 Adjusting the steering rack ball head

1 Fit the special adjusting clamp, tool No. 80704C, onto the steering rack. The clamp is item C of **FIG 9 : 10**.

2 Screw on a new ball head housing 2 (see **FIG 9 : 10**), and tighten to a torque of 30 to 36 lb ft.

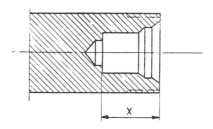

UP TO Nos :		AS FROM Nos :	
404	4,019.542	404	4,019.543
404 J	4.500.792	404 J	4.500.793
X = 22,5 mm		X = 23 mm	

FIG 9 : 5 Ball head recess depth in the end of the steering rack

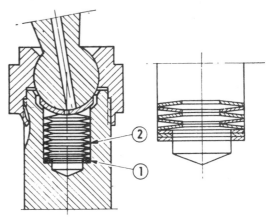

FIG 9 : 6   Rack ball head assembly

Key to Fig 9 : 6   1 Adjusting shims   2 Belleville washers

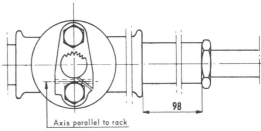

Axis parallel to rack

FIG 9 : 7 Correct position for assembling the pinion to rack and housing. The dimension 98 is in millimetres

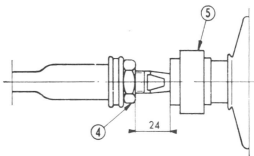

FIG 9 : 8   Lefthand connecting link assembly. The dimension 24 is in millimetres.

Key to Fig 9 : 8   4 Locknut   5 Ball head housing

3 Bring the adjusting clamp up into contact with the housing and tighten the clamp lockscrew.

4 Remove the ball head housing without disturbing the adjusting clamp and fit the ball head shell (item 4 of **FIG 9 : 11**), in place in the rack.

5 Install the ball head 5, and insert pin D into the ball head centre bore to align the shell.

6 Screw on the ball head housing 2, withdraw the pin D, and continue to screw the housing until the ball head can no longer swivel within the housing.

7 Using feeler gauges, measure the clearance between the housing 2, and the adjusting clamp C at the position X of **FIG 9 : 11**.

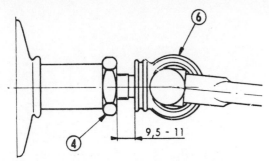

FIG 9:9 Righthand connecting link eyebolt. The threaded portion should protrude 9.5 to 11 mm from the locknut when correctly assembled.

Key to Fig 9:9   4 Eyebolt locknut   6 Eyebolt

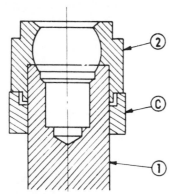

FIG 9:10 Steering rack with the adjusting clamp in position with the ball head housing tightened to the correct figure

Key to Fig 9:10   1 Steering rack   2 Ball head housing
C Adjusting clamp

8 Remove the ball head housing, ball head and ball head shell and take off the adjusting clamp.
9 Replace the ball head and shell, align with the pin D as in operation 5, place the shim thickness calculated in operation 7 plus an additional .05 mm (.002 inch) shim in the housing. Screw the housing onto the rack and torque load to 30 to 36 lb ft. The ball head should be free to swivel without slackness. Adjustment shims are available in the following sizes: .10, .15, .20 and .50 mm.

9:7 Adjusting the pinion side rack damper plunger clearance

1 Place the rack damper thrust spacer on a surface plate and position the damper plunger on the spacer as shown in **FIG 9:12.**
2 Insert the adjusting shims between the top of the spacer and the bottom of the plunger until a .20 mm (.008 inch) clearance exists between the plunger and the surface plate.
3 Install the shims on the flange and locate them on the end of the grease nipple. Screw the nylon spacer on the threaded inner end of the grease nipple to retain the shims in position.

4 Fit the damper assembly, so adjusted, to the rack housing and tighten the flange retaining screws to a torque of 7.25 to 9 lb ft.
Adjustment shims are available in .10, .20 and .50 mm sizes.

9:8 Connecting link ball joints

Dismantling:

1 Hold the connecting link in a vice and remove the circlip from the ball head cap (see **FIG 9:13**).
2 Remove in the following order: ball head cap and grease nipple, 4 Belleville washers, nylon half bearing shell, ball bolt and steel half bearing shell.

Reassembly:

1 Check and renew parts where necessary.
2 Install the steel half bearing shell in the bottom of the ball joint housing.
3 Refer to **FIG 9:13** and refit in the following order the ball bolt, nylon half bearing shell, four Belleville washers and the ball head cap.
4 Compress the Belleville washers and install a new circlip in the groove above the cap.
5 Position the ball head correctly with the pin hole in the end of the ball bolt at right angles to the connecting link axis. Lubricate the assembly.

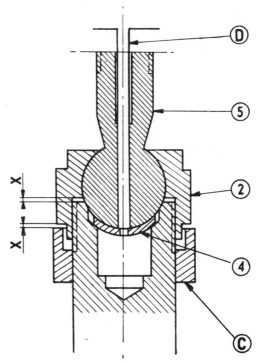

FIG 9:11 Adjusting the rack ball head assembly

Key to Fig 9:11   2 Ball head housing   4 Ball head shell
5 Ball head   **C** Adjusting clamp   **D** Aligning pin for 4
X Adjusting shim thickness

9:9 Refitting the rack and pinion unit

1 Position the rack assembly against the crossmember and fit the two attachment screws. Tighten to a torque of 22 to 32 lb ft. It will be necessary to disconnect the front engine mountings in order to apply a torque wrench to these screws. Reconnect the mountings after tightening the rack assembly screws.

2 Reconnect the steering at the flexible coupling and tighten the yoke bolt to a torque of 5.5 to 9 lb ft. Lock the bolt by peening.

3 Fit the steering connecting links in the steering arms and tighten the ball joint nuts to 36 to 40 lb ft and lock with splitpins.

4 Bring the right hand connecting link into position and fit and tighten the eye bolt and nut.

5 Adjust the front wheel alignment to .079 ± .039 inch toe-in by screwing the ball head nut on the lefthand connecting link in or out. Tighten the locknut against the ball head nut.

6 Fit and secure the rubber boots on the rack housing and connecting links.

7 Check the installation by turning the steering wheel from lock to lock.

8 Check the steering wheel position in the straight-ahead position and correct as necessary by removing and repositioning the wheel.

9:10 Road testing the steering

Drive the car at about 30 mile/hr and then take your hands off the steering wheel. The car should maintain a straight course. If the road is crowned, it may cause the car to wander towards the low side of the road and, therefore, it may be necessary to make this test straddled over the centre line. Uneven front end angles will cause the car to wander to one side.

Hold your hands lightly on the steering wheel at about 30 mile/hr to check whether any shocks are being transmitted back to the steering wheel. A constantly jiggling wheel indicates that the front wheels are out of balance. Apart from being tiring to the driver on a long journey this movement is bound to accelerate wear on every moving part of the front end.

With the car moving at about 25 mile/hr turn through 90 deg. and then release the steering wheel. It should come back to the straightahead position without any assistance from the driver. If it does not it indicates binding in the linkage, insufficient caster or insufficient steering axis inclination.

To check for misalignment, inspect the front tyres for uneven tread wear. Sharp edges felt going one way are called feather edges and are developed from sideways scuffing often due to incorrect toe-in.

9:11 Fault diagnosis

(a) Wheel wobble

1 Unbalanced wheels and tyres
2 Slack steering connections
3 Incorrect steering geometry
4 Excessive play in steering gear
5 Weak front springs
6 Worn hub bearings

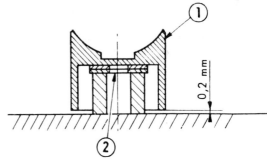

FIG 9:12   Damper plunger clearance adjustment

Key to Fig 9:12   1 Rack damper plunger   2 Adjusting shims

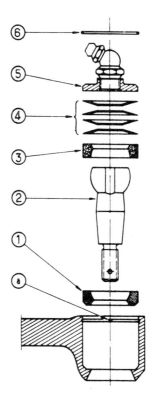

FIG 9:13   Exploded view of connecting link outer ball joint

Key to Fig 9:13   1 Steel half bearing shell   2 Ball bolt 3 Nylon half bearing shell   4 Belleville washers   5 Ball head   6 Circlip   a Ball joint body

(b) Wander

1 Check 2, 3 and 4 in (a)
2 Front suspension and rear axle mounting points out of line
3 Uneven tyre pressures
4 Uneven tyre wear
5 Weak dampers or springs

(c) Heavy steering

1 Check 3 in (a)
2 Very low tyre pressures
3 Neglected lubrication
4 Wheels out of track
5 Steering gear maladjusted
6 Excessive castor

(d) Lost motion

1 Incorrect adjustment of steering gear
2 Worn steering linkage
3 Loose wheel bearing adjustment
4 Worn kingpins or ball joints
5 Loose mountings of steering gear

CHAPTER 10

THE BRAKING SYSTEM

10:1 The description

The braking system is comprised of Bendix brake equipment operated by Lockheed hydraulic controls.

The footbrake operates through the hydraulic system. The front brakes are of the two-leading-shoe type, incorporating two single ended cylinders for each pair of brake shoes. The leading/trailing shoe rear brakes are each operated by a floating type cylinder.

The parking brake operates through a separate mechanical system, the control lever being connected to the rear brakes by cable.

The master cylinder is of the centre valve type with the reservoir screwed to the cylinder body.

Peugeot models from 1965 are equipped with Hydrovac vacuum controlled power brakes. Temperature compensated front brakes are fitted in which the front brake drums are manufactured from high thermal conductivity cast iron.

From 1969, the Hydrovac is replaced by Mastervac vacuum control and disc brakes are fitted to the front wheels.

The general layout of the three types of system can be seen in **FIGS 10:1, 10:2** and **10:3**.

10:2 Routine maintenance

Every 300 miles check the level in the master cylinder reservoir and top up if necessary.

The master cylinder reservoir has a screw cap, but before adding fluid, clean the filler cap to prevent dirt entering the reservoir. Top up the reservoir to the 'Maxi' mark with the recommended brake fluid. **Use only the correct fluid and do not use containers which have been used for other fluids.** Contamination spreads rapidly in the hydraulic system, causing a dangerous deterioriation of the rubber seals, which can cause a complete failure of the braking system.

Every 24,000 miles or 18 months, whichever comes first, the whole brake system should be drained and refilled with clean fluid.

Brake shoe adjustment

Front brakes:

1 Apply the handbrake and jack up the front of the car until the wheels are free to rotate.

2 Turn one of the two adjusters on the brake backing plate (see **FIG 10:4**), in a forward direction until the shoe is locked against the drum. Release the adjust-

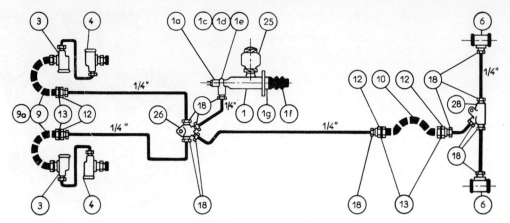

FIG 10:1   Brake system layout, early models, from May 1960

Key to Fig 10:1   1 Master cylinder   3/4 Front wheel cylinders   6 Rear wheel cylinders   9/10 Flexible pipes   25 Reservoir

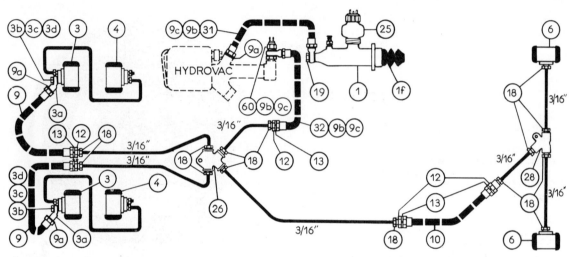

FIG 10:2   Brake system layout, from 1965

Key to Fig 10:2   1 Master cylinder   3/4 Front wheel cylinders   6 Rear wheel cylinders   9/10 Flexible pipes

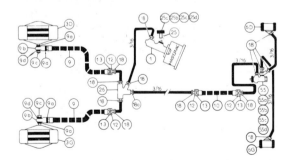

FIG 10:3   Brake system layout, from 1969

Key to Fig 10:3   1 Master cylinder   3D and 3G Brake calipers   6D and 6G Rear wheel cylinders   9/10 Flexible hoses   25 Reservoir   55 Regulator valve assembly

ment in the reverse direction until the wheel is just free to rotate.

3 Repeat this operation on the other adjuster of the same wheel. Apply the foot brake several times and again check the wheel for free rotation.

4 Carry out the same operations on the other front wheel before lowering the car to the ground.

Rear brakes:

1 Chock the front wheels securely, jack up the rear of the car and release the handbrake.

2 Turn the front square-headed adjustment bolt in a forward direction until the shoe is in contact with the drum. Turn the adjuster in the reverse direction until the wheel is just free to rotate.

3 Rotate the rear square-headed adjustment bolt in a rearward direction until the brake shoe is in contact

with the drum, then rotate in a forward direction until the drum is just free to rotate.

4 Carry out the procedures for operation 2 and 3 on the other rear wheel, apply the foot brake pedal several times and check for free rotation of the rear wheels.

5 Lower the rear of the car to the ground.

Preventative maintenance:

Regularly examine friction pads (cars with disc brakes), brake linings and all pipes, unions and hoses for wear, damage or deterioration. Never use anything but the recommended fluid for topping up the brakes. Do not leave brake fluid in unsealed containers as it will absorb moisture which can be dangerous.

It is best to discard fluid drained from the system or after bleeding. Observe absolute cleanliness when working on all parts of the hydraulic system.

10:3 Brake drums and brake shoes

The brake drums used on servo controlled systems are made of high thermal conductivity cast iron and can be identified by an oval shaped mark on the drum (see **FIG 10:5**). Brake drums used for previous systems must on no account be used on temperature compensated brakes.

The drums are balanced by the installation of a counterweight and when removing the drums from the hub they should always be marked to ensure correct reassembly. The hubs can be removed, after removing the road wheels, by taking out the three countersunk screws.

Slight ovality or scoring can be removed by refacing the brake drums, providing the internal diameter is not increased by more than 1 mm.

Front brake shoe removal:

Righthand brake:

1 Jack up the front of the car and remove the road wheel.

2 Mark the brake drum position in relation to the hub with chalk, to facilitate correct reassembly.

3 Remove the brake drum by unscrewing the three countersunk screws.

4 Remove both outer springs, using a pair of pliers to stretch them and unhook them from the brake shoes.

5 Remove both inner springs by placing the blade of a screwdriver on the end of the spring hook, and tapping the handle.

6 Remove the lateral springs and the brake shoes.

Lefthand brake:

Removing and reassembling the inner return springs of the brake shoes requires the use of a special tool (see **FIG 10:6**), which can be obtained from Peugeot service agents.

To remove the brake shoes repeat operations 1 to 4 as for the righthand brake shoes and then proceed as follows:

1 Engage hook 'a' of the tool under a spring wire and rotate the tool gently in the direction indicated in **FIG 10:7,** until the hook disengages itself from its fixed point.

2 Insert a screwdriver between the spring hook and the fixed point and remove the spring.

FIG 10:4   Brake shoe adjustment

FIG 10:5   Brake drum identification

Key to Fig 10:5 1 Oval-shaped mark indicating high thermal conductivity brake drum 2 Balancing counter-weight

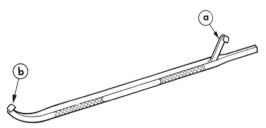

FIG 10:6   Brake spring tool, No. 8.0802. This tool is required for removing and refitting the inner return springs of the front brake shoes

FIG 10:7 Method of removing inner springs (lefthand front brake)

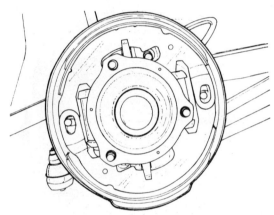

FIG 10:8 Positioning the brake shoes against the brake plate

3 Remove the lateral springs and then the brake shoes.
    After the brake shoes have been removed it is advisable to tie a length of wire around the brake cylinder and piston to prevent displacement of the piston.

Relining brake shoes:

If the linings are worn down to the rivets, renewal is necessary. It is not recommended that owners should reline brake shoes themselves. It is important that the linings should be perfectly bedded down on the shoes and then ground to perfect concentricity with the brake drums. For this reason it is best to obtain sets of replacement shoes already lined. Do not fit odd shoes and do not mix lining materials or unbalanced braking will result.
    Do not allow oil, grease or paint to come into contact with the brake shoe linings. If the original linings are contaminated with oil or grease do not attempt to clean them with solvents as nothing useful can be achieved.

Front brake shoe reassembly:
Righthand front brake:

1 Remove the wire from around the brake cylinder and piston.
2 Position both brake shoes against the brake plate and secure with the lateral springs. The offset end of the brake shoe should be located outside the brake plate and positioned as follows:
    Towards the front for the upper brake shoe.
    Towards the rear for the lower brake shoe.
    This positioning can be clearly seen in the view of the brake drum and shoes in FIG 10:8.
3 Install both inner springs, with the aid of the special tool, in the following manner:
    Position the springs between the brake shoes and the brake plate and engage the small hook of each spring in the corresponding holes of the brake shoes.
    Engage the hook 'b' of the brake tool under the fixed point and catch the spring hook with the hook of the tool (see FIG 10:9).
4 Rotate the tool around the fixed point, at the same time pulling to secure the spring. Remove the tool.
5 The larger hooks of the inner springs may be closed slightly after fitting if necessary.
6 Install both outer springs by engaging the tool hook 'b' in the spring hook and pulling until the spring hook can be engaged.
7 Refit brake drum to the hub, ensuring that the alignment marks made during dismantling are aligned.

FIG 10:9 Positioning the inner springs (righthand front brake)

Refit the road wheel before lowering the car to the ground, adjust the brakes as detailed in **Section 10:2.**

Reassembling lefthand front brake:

1 Remove the wire from around the brake cylinder and piston.
2 Position the brake shoes against the brake plate and secure with the lateral springs. The offset end of the brake shoes should be located in the same manner as for the righthand brake, i.e.
Towards the front for the upper brake shoe.
Towards the rear for the lower brake shoe.
3 Install both inner springs, using the brake tool, in the following manner:
Position the springs between the brake shoes and the brake plate and engage the small hook of each spring in the corresponding holes in the brake shoes.
Engage the tool, hook 'a', in the spring hook and rotate tool around the fixed point. At the same time pull on the tool until it is possible to engage the spring hook. Remove the tool.
4 Install the outer springs. The larger hooks of the inner springs may be closed slightly after fitting if necessary.
5 Refit the brake drum to the hub and adjust the brakes.

Brake shoe springs:

All the brake shoe inner return springs are identical and incorporate 26 turns.

The outer return springs (see item 2 of **FIG 10:10**), are different for the left- and righthand brakes. The spring hook position on the spring differs, to prevent chafing of the spring wire against the brake cylinder boot (see **FIG 10:10**).

10:4 Checking the brake pedal travel

1 Start the engine and accelerate two or three times in succession to obtain the maximum vacuum in the Hydrovac unit.
2 Run the engine at idling speed and measure the height of the brake pedal from the floor.
3 Depress the brake pedal until the vacuum is gone from the Hydrovac unit. At this point the effort required to depress the pedal increases suddenly.
4 Hold the pedal in the depressed position and again measure the height of the pedal from the floor.
5 The movement of the pedal can now be calculated, and this should not exceed 60 mm (approx. 2.4 inches).
6 If the pedal movement is more than this it is an indication that the brakes need adjusting. If the pedal movement is still excessive after adjusting the brakes the brake system should be bled.

10:5 Hydraulic equipment

The hydraulic equipment fitted to the Peugeot 404 includes (after 1965), a Hydrovac vacuum controlled power brake unit, operated by the master cylinder.

The Hydrovac is a sealed unit and no dismantling is permitted or required, apart from changing the filter element. The element must be replaced with a new item as no cleaning or oiling is permissible. The Hydrovac unit is shown in **FIG 10:11.**

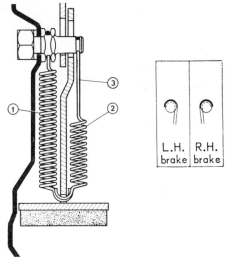

FIG 10:10   Brake shoe return springs
Key to Fig 10:10   1 Inner springs   2 Outer springs. Note that the spring hook for lefthand and righthand brake is different, to prevent chafing of the wire 3, against the brake cylinder

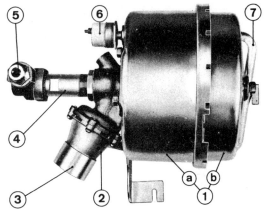

FIG 10:11   The Hydrovac unit
Key to Fig 10:11   1 Vacuum cylinder   2 Control valve 3 Air intake filter   4 Slave hydraulic cylinder   5 Residual pressure valve connection   6 Pressure switch for warning light

Servo assistance is available only when the engine is running, and although braking efficiency is not in any way impaired, considerably greater pressure will be required on the pedal when running with the engine stopped. A vacuum operated pressure switch is used to indicate possible failure of the brake assister system. This lights a lamp on the facia when the vacuum in the reservoir is less than 5 lb/sq inch.

The master cylinder and the front and rear wheel cylinders are of conventional design and construction and exploded views of these components can be seen in **FIGS 10:12, 10:12a, 10:13** and **10:14.**

All hydraulic brake parts should be washed in commercial alcohol, methylated spirits or approved brake fluid.

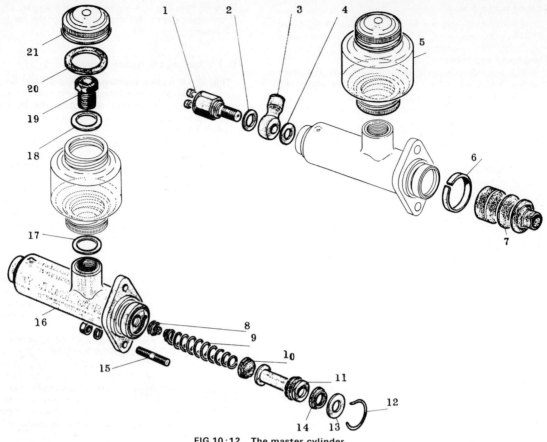

FIG 10:12   The master cylinder

Key to Fig 10:12   1 Stoplight switch   2 Washer   3 Banjo connection   4 Washer   5 Reservoir   6 Spring clip   7 Dust cover   8 Spring seat   9 Spring   10 Primary piston seal   11 Piston   12 Circlip   13 Stop plate   14 Secondary piston seal   15 Stud   16 Master cylinder body   17 Sealing ring   18 Sealing ring   19 Reservoir screw   20 Gasket   21 Cap

Do not use mineral oils, or cleaning fluid extracted from mineral oils, e.g., petrol, paraffin, carbon tetra-chloride, etc., as they will cause the rubber seals to swell and become ineffective. The slightest trace of mineral oil could soon render the brakes inoperative. Methylated spirits or commercial alcohol must always be used for flushing out the system, washing brake housings, components and any containers that come into contact with brake fluid.

Any foreign matter should be washed away from components with methylated spirits or commercial alcohol. If foreign matter finds its way into the system it may score the pistons and damage the seals, and will consequently render the brakes either wholly or partly inoperative.

Pistons and seals should be carefully stored away from grease or oils and handled carefully at all times. The seals should be inspected carefully before fitting, even if they are new.

See that the sealing lips are perfectly formed, concentric with the bore of the seal, free from knife edges, surface blemishes or marks. Any seal that is not perfect, no matter how minute the blemish may be, should be rejected. Seals should not be turned inside out when inspecting them, since this strains the surface skin and may eventually lead to a failure.

All pistons and housings must be carefully inspected before assembly. Any imperfections or scores on a piston or cylinder bore may provide a track for fluid leaks under pressure, and any damaged parts must be discarded. Parts must be handled very carefully to avoid any possibility of accidental scoring.

Prior to assembly, immerse the components and parts in approved brake fluid to facilitate fitting and provide initial lubrication for working surfaces.

Removing a flexible hose:

Never try to release a flexible hose by turning the ends with a spanner. The correct procedure is as follows:

Unscrew the metal pipeline union nut from its connection with the hose. Hold the adjacent hexagon on the hose with a spanner and remove the locknut which secures the hose to the bracket. The hose can now be turned without twisting the flexible part, by using a spanner on the hexagon on the other end.

Front brake hoses:

Front brake hoses are connected to the front brake cylinders by means of a swivel connector and when replacing or renewing a hose the following procedure should be adopted:

1 The hose connector should be at the lower part of the front cylinder, and slanted about 45 deg. above the horizontal (see item 1 of **FIG 10:15**).

2 The connecting tube, item 2, should be installed as shown.

3 The bleed screw, item 3, should be situated at the top of the rear cylinder.

10:6 Handbrake adjustment

The handbrake is adjusted automatically with the footbrake, and normally no other adjustment is required. If there is still too much travel after adjustment of the brakes, suspect worn brake linings or a stretched handbrake cable. Examine the linings and fit replacement shoes if they are worn. Check the action of the handbrake again and if there is still too much movement before the brakes are applied, it may be adjusted as follows:

1 Chock the front wheels, jack up the rear of the car and check the adjustment of the rear brake shoes with the handbrake in the off position.

2 Remove the clevis pins from both rear brake cables at the equalizer bar at the front end of the rear cables.

3 Set the equalizer bar parallel to the cross centre line of the car with the handbrake in the fully off position.

4 Release the locknuts and adjust both cables (see **FIG 10:16**), so that the clevis pins will engage their respective holes in the equalizer bar without altering the position of the bar, or imposing a strain on the cables. Tighten the locknuts and fit new splitpins in the clevis pins.

5 Check that the rear shoes are not dragging on the rear brake drums and lower the rear of the car to the ground.

10:7 Bleeding the hydraulic system

This is not routine maintenance and should only be necessary if air has entered the hydraulic system because parts have been dismantled, or because the fluid level in the master cylinder reservoir has dropped so low that air has been drawn in.

Before bleeding the hydraulic system, the following points should be observed:

1 Examine the master cylinder reservoir cap and ensure that the vent hole is clear.

2 The fluid in the reservoir should be up to the 'Maxi' mark.

3 All unions and connections should be checked for tightness and freedom from leaks. Also check the condition of flexible hoses.

Bleeding the system:

1 Clean the area around the bleed valves. The bleed valves on the rear wheel cylinders are the easier to reach and it is suggested that these should be bled first. If these are thoroughly done it may not be necessary to do the front wheels.

2 Remove the rubber cap on the bleed valve and fit a rubber or transparent tube on the valve.

3 Place the end of the tube in a jar containing clean brake fluid. Keep the end of the tube beneath the surface of the fluid during the bleeding operation.

4 Open the bleed valve half a turn and depress the brake pedal fully to the floor, ensuring that the movement is not restricted by any undue thickness of floor

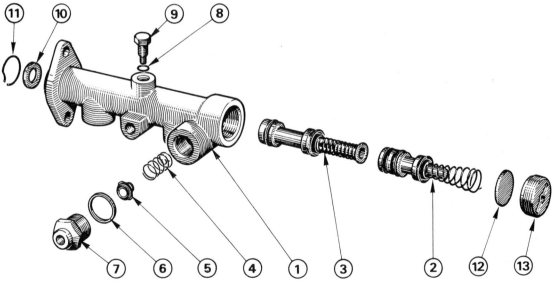

FIG 10:12a Tandem master cylinder fitted to some export vehicles

Key to Fig 10:12a   1 Master cylinder body   2 Secondary piston assembly   3 Primary piston assembly   4 Valve spring
5 Residual pressure valve   6 Copper gasket   7 Valve support and connector   8 Seal ring   9 Stop screw   10 Stop washer
11 Snap ring   12 Copper gasket   13 Threaded plug

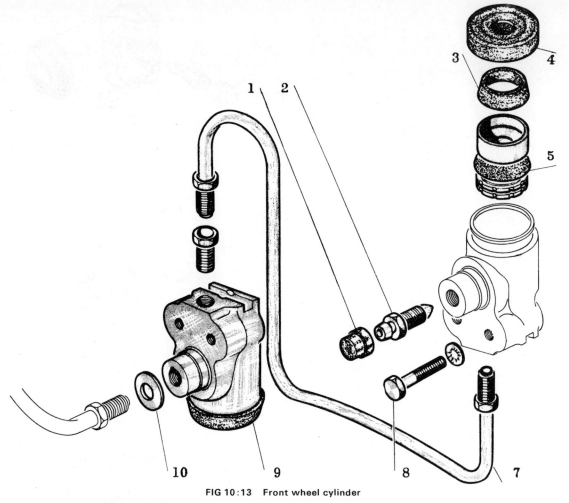

FIG 10:13 Front wheel cylinder

Key to Fig 10:13   1 Bleed valve cap   2 Bleed valve   3 Leather washer   4 Dust cap   5 Piston   7 Interconnecting pipe
8 Securing screw   9 Front wheel cylinder   10 Washer

covering. Quickly release the pedal and then pause for an instant to ensure full recuperation of the master cylinder. Repeat this operation several times. For each stroke of the brake pedal, fluid and/or air should be discharged from the tube. If neither fluid nor air is discharged, the bleed valve is not properly open or there is a blockage in the pipeline.

5 Continue to operate the brake pedal until air bubbles cease to emerge from the tube. It is important that the fluid level in the master cylinder reservoir is maintained during the bleeding operation, otherwise air may be drawn through the surface of the fluid into the master cylinder. Do not replenish the master cylinder reservoir with fluid drained from the system as this may be contaminated or aerated.

6 When, with each stroke of the brake pedal, fluid alone is pumped out of the bleed valve, close the valve with the pedal fully depressed. Tighten the bleed valve to a torque of 9 to 10 lb ft.

7 Repeat the operation on the other wheels as necessary.

8 Refill the reservoir to the 'Maxi' mark and replace the cap.

9 Check the action of the brakes on a road test.

Note that during the bleeding operation, the vacuum in the servo unit will gradually be destroyed and the effort required for one complete depression of the pedal will progressively get greater and greater. The brakes can still be bled quite satisfactorily when the servo is in this condition.

Hydraulic fluid:

On early models before servo assistance and temperature compensated brakes were fitted, the systems were filled with brake fluid HD.31 or HD.65. It is permissible to mix these fluids together.

Lockheed HD.43* fluid is used for all cars equipped with temperature compensated brakes. This fluid must

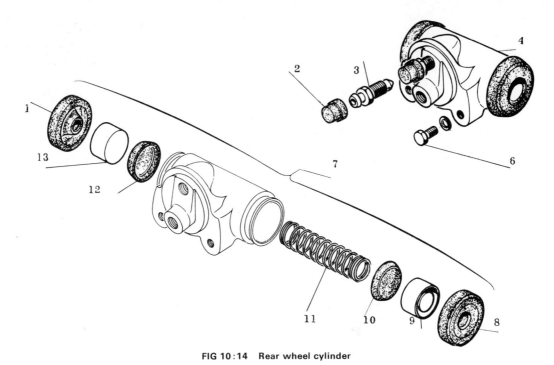

FIG 10:14   Rear wheel cylinder

Key to Fig 10:14   1 Piston cap   2 Bleed valve cap   3 Bleed valve   4 Rear wheel cylinder assembly   6 Screw
7 Exploded view of rear wheel cylinder   8 Piston cap   9 Piston   10 Leather washer   11 Spring   12 Leather washer
13 Piston

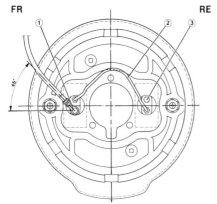

FIG 10:15   Front brake hose and connecting tube assembly

Key to Fig 10:15   1 Swivel hose connector
2 Interconnecting pipe   3 Bleed screw

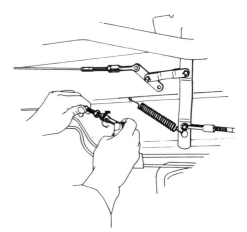

FIG 10:16   Adjusting the handbrake controls

never be mixed with any other fluid. This fluid may be used on early systems after the HD.31 or HD.65 has been drained and the system flushed through.

10:8 Disc front brakes

As mentioned earlier the braking system was modified in 1969 to include disc brakes on the front wheels. The construction of these assemblies is clearly shown in the exploded views given in **FIG 10:17** and reference to this

should assist in any dismantling which may become necessary. It is stressed that for the purpose of illustration the caliper is shown split into two halves but this should NEVER be done other than by qualified service personnel.

Disc brakes are self-adjusting and should require no maintenance other than renewal of the friction pads as soon as they are worn down to a thickness of 2.5 mm. Note that all the pads on the same axle should be changed and not just those that have worn.

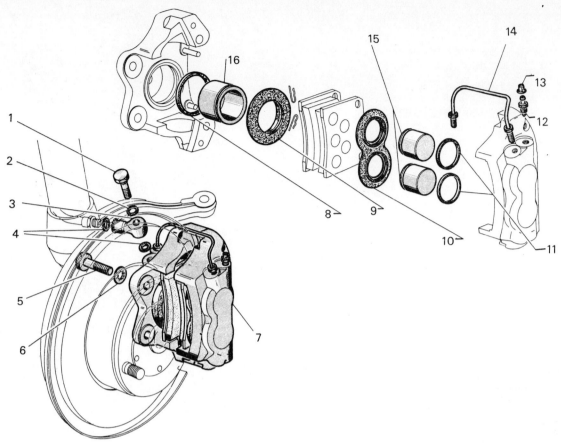

FIG 10:17   Components of front brake caliper assembly

Key to Fig 10:17   1 Hollow bolt   2 Washer   3 Banjo union   4 Washer   5 Bolt   6 Lockwasher   7 Caliper   8 Washer
9 Rubber seal   10 Rubber seal   11 Washer   12 Bleed screw   13 Cap   14 Connecting pipe   15 Pistons   16 Piston

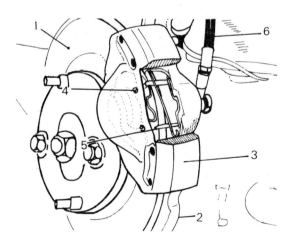

FIG 10:18   Removing brake pads

Key to Fig 10:18   1 Disc   2 Shield   3 Caliper
4 Upper retaining pin   5 Lower retaining pin   6 Fluid
supply pipe

Renewing brake pads (see FIG 10:18)

Jack up the front of the car and remove the two road wheels. Carefully clean the calipers with dry rags, taking care not to dislodge or damage the rubber seals.

Attach a length of tube to the bleed screw and immerse the free end in a clean glass jar containing a quantity of fluid.

Remove the retaining spring of the pad pins and withdraw the pins from the inboard side. Slacken the bleed screw one turn.

Using a suitable tool as a lever push the single piston on the inboard side into its bore and also the two pistons on the outboard side. This will cause the expulsion of a small quantity of brake fluid into the jar. Tighten up the bleed screw and remove the tube.

Remove the pads and check the caliper assembly for tightness. Inspect the brake disc and make sure that it is not unduly scored. Check also the disc run-out, which must not exceed .10 mm. Badly scored or distorted discs should be renewed. Any cleaning necessary on the disc should be done with trichlorethylene.

Fit new pads on both sides of the disc and replace the retaining pins from the inboard side. Refit the retaining springs, taking care not to damage the rubber seal on the inner piston. When fitting the springs make sure that the straight end which goes through the pin, is positioned inward facing the rubber seal and the round end outward away from the seal.

Check that the bleed screws are tight, then operate the brake pedal several times until a solid resistance is felt, this will indicate that any gaps between piston and pad or pad and disc have been taken up.

Check the fluid level in the reservoir and top up if necessary with Lockheed 43*.

Bleeding the brakes:

This has already been described in **Section 10:7** and the procedure when disc brakes are fitted remains the same.

If when bleeding the rear brakes the pedal suddenly becomes 'hard', this indicates that the brake pressure regulator has become operative usually due to over vigorous application of the pedal. To rectify this condition proceed as follows:

Tighten up the rear bleed screws and release the hand brake with a sudden jerk. This will cause the rear shoes to move back from the drums and make a return flow of fluid in the pipes which in turn causes the pressure limiter ball balve of the brake regulator to lift off its seat. Pull on the hand brake again and continue the bleeding operation.

When bleeding the front brakes in order to expel any air which may have been trapped in the bottom cylinder, complete the bleeding as follows:

Tighten the bleed screw and hold the pedal firmly down for about 10 seconds then slacken off the bleed screw without releasing the pedal. Tighten the screw and release the pedal. Repeat until no more air bubbles are visible.

10:9 Fault diagnosis

(a) 'Spongy pedal'

1 Leak in the system
2 Worn master cylinder
3 Leaking wheel cylinders
4 Air in the system

(b) Excessive pedal movement

1 Check 1 and 4 in (a)
2 Excessive lining wear
3 Very low fluid level in reservoir

(c) Brakes grab or pull to one side

1 Brake backplate loose
2 Scored, cracked or distorted drum
3 High spots on drum
4 Unbalanced shoe adjustment
5 Wet or oily linings
6 Worn steering connections
7 Front suspension or rear axle anchorages loose
8 Mixed linings of different grades
9 Uneven tyre pressures
10 Broken shoe return springs
11 Seized handbrake cable(s)

NOTES

CHAPTER 11

THE ELECTRICAL SYSTEM

11:1 Description

All models covered by this manual have a 12-volt system in which the negative battery terminal is earthed. There are three units in the regulator box to control the charging circuit; a cut-out, a current regulator and a voltage regulator. The regulator is a sealed unit and is not fitted with any adjustment device.

There are wiring diagrams in the Technical Data at the end of this Manual to enable those with electrical experience to trace and correct wiring faults.

The headlamps are of the assymetric beam type and may be manufactured by either Marchal, Ducellier or Cibie.

The battery is mounted on the lefthand side of the engine compartment. A battery lock switch is fitted on the negative terminal and to switch off the battery the wing nuts should be unscrewed two turns.

The generator which may be of either Paris-Rhone or Ducellier manufacture has a normal output of 23 amps.

The starter motor, either Ducellier or Paris-Rhone, is of the positive electro-magnetic type and is attached to the engine at three points, two on the clutch housing and one on the cylinder block.

Instructions for the maintenance of the electrical equipment will be found in this chapter, but it must be stressed that it is not sensible to try to repair anything which is seriously defective, either mechanically or electrically. Any such equipment should be replaced by new units obtainable at Peugeot service stations.

11:2 The battery

The battery is a conventional lead/acid type with a 55 amp/hr capacity and is negatively earthed. Provided the battery is properly maintained it will function satisfactorily between the temperature extremes of winter and summer.

To maintain the performance of the battery at its maximum it is essential to carry out the following operations.

Remove the vent plugs and check the level of the electrolyte in each of the six cells. Do not place the vent plugs on any part of the car, as they will be wet with acid. Distilled water should be added to each cell as required, to bring the level of the electrolyte to just above the separators, and no more. Do not overfill, as the electrolyte may be sprayed out during charging. Never add acid

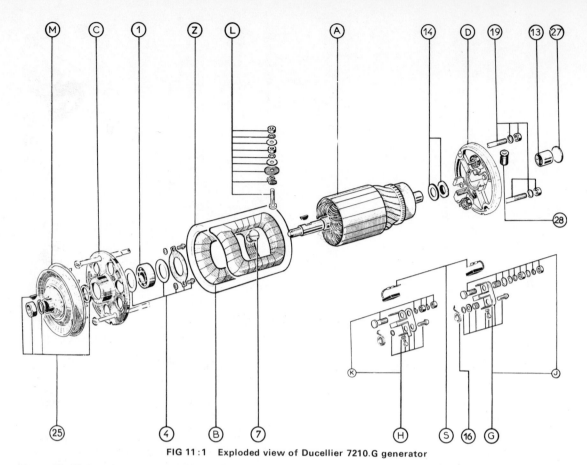

FIG 11:1   Exploded view of Ducellier 7210.G generator

Key to Fig 11:1   **A** Armature   **B** Field coil   **C** Drive end frame   **D** Commutator end frame   **S** Brushes   **J** Insulated terminal   **K** Neutral point terminal   **L** Field terminal   **M** Pulley   **Z** Body   1 Bearing   4 Control bearing   7 Neutral pole screw   10 Shim   13 Graphite ring   14 Washers   16 Brush spring   19 Mounting leads   25 Pulley mounting assembly   28 Lubricator

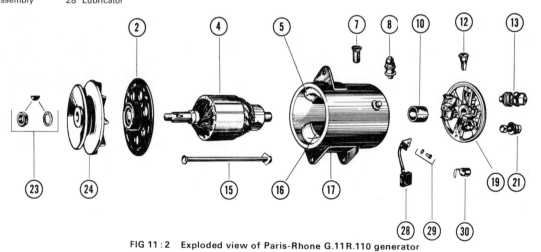

FIG 11:2   Exploded view of Paris-Rhone G.11R.110 generator

Key to Fig 11:2   2 Drive end bearing cap   4 Armature   5 Field coils   7 Polepiece screw   8 EXC terminal assembly   10 Commutator end bush   12 Lubricator   13 DYN terminal assembly   15 Assembly screw   16 Polepiece   17 Yoke   19 Commutator end cover   21 M terminal assembly   23 Pulley attachment fitting   24 Drive pulley   28 Commutator brush   29 Brush lead attachment   30 Brush spring

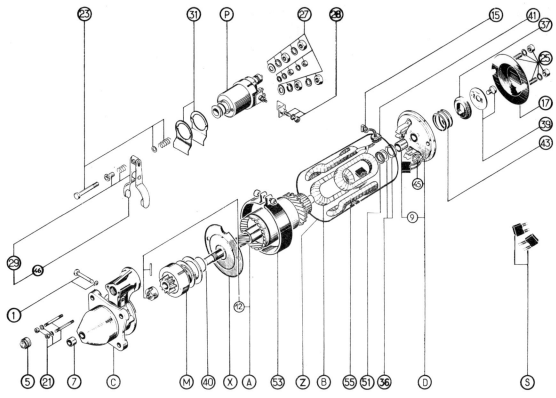

FIG 11 : 3   Exploded view of Ducellier type **6081** starter

Key to Fig 11 : 3   **A** Armature   **B** Field coil   **C** Drive end frame   **D** Commutator end frame   **S** Set of brushes
J Insulated terminal   **M** Bendix drive   **P** Solenoid   **Z** Body   1 Fork pin   5 Solenoid plug   7 Graphite ring   9 Graphite
ring   12 Pinion stop   15 Inducer outlet connection   17 Bearing cap   21 Mounting bolts   23 Adjusting rod
25 Mounting leads   27 Solenoid terminals   29 Fork   31 Gasket   36 Collector ring   37 Brake pad   39 Parts of brake
pad   41 Wire guard   43 Brake spring   45 Brush spring   46 Fork pad   55 Pole shoe screw

when topping up the battery. Only water evaporates as a result of charging and discharging, and if this is not replaced, sections of the plates will become exposed to the air, causing the plates to sulphate and consequently impair the efficiency of the battery. Abnormal evaporation is an indication that the battery is being overcharged. If excessive topping up is necessary to keep the level of the electrolyte correct, the current-voltage controller should be checked for correct operation.

When replacing the vent plugs, ensure that they are screwed down firmly, otherwise leakage of the electrolyte may occur.

The battery and its surrounding parts must be kept clean and dry, particularly the battery top. Any accumulation of dirt and acid will cause electrical leakage between the terminal lugs.

If electrolyte has spilled over and corrosion has taken place, remove the battery and thoroughly clean it and its surrounding parts. Clean by washing the parts with a solution of ammonia or soda, and after it has stopped foaming flush off with clean water. Dry thoroughly and repaint any affected paintwork with acid resisting paint.

Before reconnecting the battery terminals, apply a coating of petroleum jelly over the terminals and terminal lugs. High electrical resistance due to corrosion at the terminal posts is often responsible for lack of sufficient current to operate the starter.

Test the condition of the cells after topping up electrolyte with distilled water to the top of the separators. **Never add neat acid. If it is necessary to make new electrolyte due to loss by spillage, add sulphuric acid to distilled water. It is highly dangerous to add water to acid.**

To test the condition of the cells use an hydrometer to check the specific gravity of the electrolyte. A reading of 1.270 indicates a fully charged battery, one of 1.175 indicates a battery in a low state of charge.

All six cells should read approximately the same. If one differs radically from the others it may be due to an internal fault or to spilling or leakage of the electrolyte.

If the battery is in a low state of charge, take the car for a long daylight run or put the battery on a charger at 4 amps until it gasses freely. When putting a battery on charge, take out the vent plugs and refrain from using naked lights when it is charging. If the battery is to stand for a long period without use, give it a freshening up charge every month, as a battery left in a discharged condition will soon become ruined.

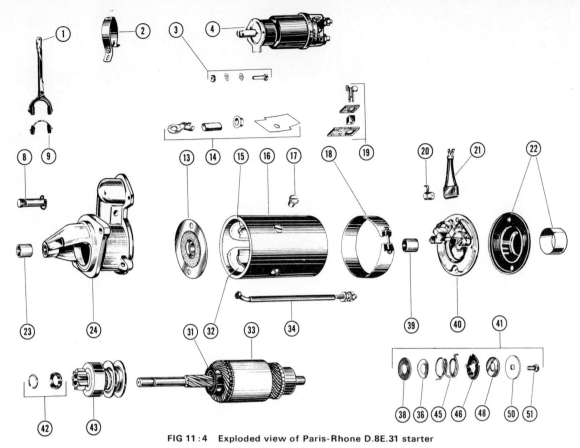

FIG 11 : 4   Exploded view of Paris-Rhone D.8E.31 starter

Key to Fig 11 : 4   1 Lever   2 Solenoid collar   3 Solenoid securing screw   4 Solenoid   8 Lever spindle   9 Lever shoes   13 Centre bush carrier plate   14 Insulating guide   15 Polepiece   16 Yoke   17 Polepiece securing screw   18 Brush cover band   19 Brush lead guide   20 Brush spring   21 Brush   22 Dust cap   23 Drive end bush   24 Drive end housing   32 Field coil   33 Armature   34 Assembly belt   39 Commutator end bush   40 Commutator end cap   41 Armature overrun brake parts   42 Pinion stop   43 Pinion assembly   38 Bakelite washers   36 Spring steel washer   45 Brake spring   46 Brake spring plate   48 Steel washer   50 Steel washer   51 Screw

11 : 3   The charging system

The charging system has a regulator, manufactured by either Paris-Rhone or Ducellier, to control the output of the generator, which again may be either Paris-Rhone or Ducellier. In practice, the charging rate increases when the battery is discharged and decreases when it is charged. The charging rate may be cut down to a very low rate when the battery is fully charged.

Unfortunately, very few specifications are available for servicing these units. In fact, the regulator is a sealed unit and no adjustments are possible. Exploded views are provided for the generators (see **FIGS 11 : 1** and **11 : 2**), as a guide for dismantling and reassembly.

To test the charging system, crank the engine with the ignition switch off in order to discharge the battery slightly. (On cars with an ignition key-type starter switch, it will be necessary to remove the high-tension wire from the centre of the distributor cap to prevent the engine starting).

Now start the engine and note the charging rate. On a car without an ammeter, it is necessary to insert an ammeter in the charging circuit. As the engine is run for a short period, the charging rate should decrease with a regulator that is controlling correctly. If the ammeter does not show any charge after the above test, it is an indication that either the generator or the regulator is at fault.

To isolate the trouble, disconnect the regulator from the circuit and energize the generator field. If the generator now charges, the trouble is in the regulator. If the generator does not charge with the regulator out of the circuit the fault is in the generator. In every case in which the generator is burned out, the regulator should be replaced as well, as it obviously did not control the output of the generator. Do not race the engine with the regulator out of the circuit as the generator will be operating without control.

To energize the field with cars equipped with either Paris-Rhone or Ducellier regulators, connect a jumper wire from the EXC terminal on the regulator to the DYN terminal.

If the generator output is excessive, the trouble can be caused by the regulator points being welded together or by a short circuit in a field wire. In either case, there is no control, and the generator is running wide open.

To test for this type of trouble, it must be remembered that there are two basic types of field circuits, one earthed at the regulator and one supplied with current at the regulator. By removing the field wire from the regulator, the generator can be isolated. If the generator still charges with the field wire removed, then the earth or short is in the generator itself.

Another generator check can be made by removing the cover band. If the inner surface of the band is spotted with a layer of solder, this indicates that the generator has been overloaded, and the solder from the commutator slots has melted. This would lead to an open circuit of the armature coils.

Voltage losses due to poor connections, cause an increase of operating voltage because the generator tries to overcome the added resistance of the circuit by forcing current through at a higher voltage. When the voltage increases, the regulator returns it to normal by regulating the field. Therefore, even though the battery is in a low state of charge, the generator output remains low.

Commutator servicing:

Examine the generator commutator for pitting and wear. One in good condition will be smooth and free from burned segments. Clean with a rag moistened with petrol. If necessary refinish as follows:

Clean and polish the surface of the commutator, using very fine glasspaper. **Do not use emerycloth.** Clean out between the segments on completion.

Visual inspection may determine the cause of armature failure. Breaks in the armature windings cause burnt commutator segments. Short circuited windings are discoloured by overheating, with badly burned commutator segments.

The armature:

Apart from cleaning the commutator as described previously, there is little which can be done to the armature itself. **Never try to straighten a bent shaft and do not machine the armature core.** Armature windings are tested with specialized equipment which is not normally available to the car owner. The only check for a suspected faulty armature which he can carry out is to substitute an armature which is known to be serviceable.

Servicing brushes:

Check for sticking of the brushes in their holders and for excessive brush wear.

To free sticking brushes, clean all carbon deposits away and if necessary, ease the brushes by lightly polishing the sides with a fine cut file. Make sure that the brushes are replaced in their original positions.

When renewing brushes they can be bedded-in by placing a strip of fine grade glasspaper around the commutator and rotating the commutator and glasspaper by hand.

11 : 4 The starters

The starter fitted to the Peugeot 404 may be either a Paris-Rhone type D8E.31 or a Ducellier 6081. As for the

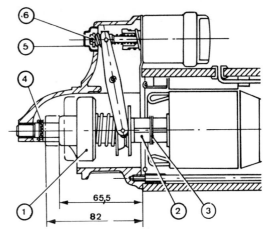

FIG 11 : 5   Starter drive and solenoid — Ducellier

Key to Fig 11 : 5   1 Pinion   2 Spacer   3 Washer   4 Stop nut   5 Plug   6 Adjusting nut

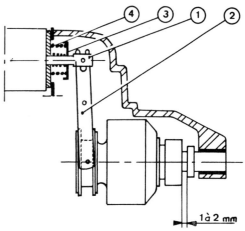

FIG 11 : 6   Starter drive and solenoid — Paris Rhone

Key to Fig 11 : 6   1 Yoke   2 Controlling fork   3 Backing cup   4 Plunger

generator and regulator, very few specifications are available for servicing the starters, but exploded views of both types are shown in **FIGS 11 : 3** and **11 : 4**, and these will help during dismantling and reassembly.

No routine lubrication is required as all the bushes are of the self-lubricating type.

Servicing brushes:

Check for sticking of the brushes in their holders and for excessive brush wear. The brushes should be replaced if their length is less than 8 mm (.315 inch).

To free sticking brushes, clean all carbon deposits away and if necessary, ease the brushes by lightly polishing the sides with a fine cut file. Make sure that the brushes are replaced in their original positions.

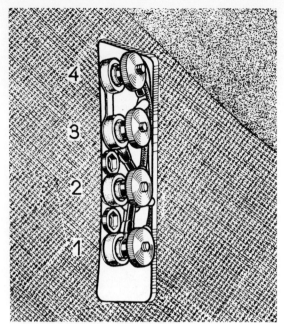

FIG 11 : 7   Fuse block and fuses

Key to Fig 11 : 7   1 10 amp fuse   2 18 amp fuse
3 10 amp fuse   4 10 amp fuse

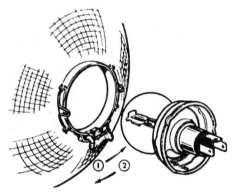

FIG 11 : 8   Changing from lefthand to righthand traffic

Key to Fig 11 : 8   1 Move to right for lefthand drive traffic
2 Move to the left for righthand drive traffic

When renewing brushes, they can be bedded-in by placing a strip of fine grade glasspaper around the commutator and rotating the commutator and glasspaper by hand.

Commutator:

Examine the starter commutator for pitting and wear and also for ovality, which should not exceed .05 mm. The commutator can be cleaned with a petrol moistened rag or refinished by using a strip of very fine glasspaper. Clean out between the segments on completion.

Starter adjustment (Ducellier):
Starter drive::

Refer to **FIG 11 : 5** and check the setting and movement of the pinion 1. Two dimensions are shown, giving the pinion position at rest and in engagement.

The rest position (65.5 mm) may be adjusted by adding or removing washers 3 behind the spacer 2. The engaged position (82 mm) can be obtained by adjusting the stop nut 4. Do not forget to refit the locking pin.

Solenoid:

The following adjustment is used to take up the longitudinal play of the drive in the free position.

Refer to **FIG 11 : 5** and remove the plug 5. Slacken the adjusting nut 6, completely and then tighten progressively until all the longitudinal play has disappeared. Unscrew the adjusting nut one quarter of a turn and reinstall the plug.

Starter adjustment (Paris-Rhone):

To adjust the clearance between the front stop and the drive pinion in the actuated position, proceed as follows:
1 Operate the starter switch under reduced voltage (10 volts) by energizing the two small terminals. The drive will then come up to the actuated position, but will not rotate the starter.
2 Push the armature and drive backwards to take up any clearance.
3 Refer to **FIG 11 : 6** and check that the clearance between the pinion and the front stop is 1 to 2 mm (.04 to .08 inch).
4 To adjust the clearance, first depress the backing cup 3, of the return spring of the plunger 4.
5 Adjust the position of the controlling fork 2, by adjusting the yoke 1.

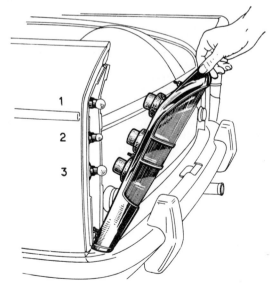

FIG 11 : 9   An early type rear light assembly

Key to Fig 11 : 9   1 Indicator light   2 Rear light
3 Stoplight

While doing this adjustment, the solenoid should not remain energized for more than a few seconds to avoid deterioration of the windings.

11:5 Fuses and fuse ratings

The electrical circuit contains four fuses which are installed on a board under the dashboard on the lefthand side. The fuses are numbered 1 to 4 and protect the following circuits:

Fuse No. 1—The head and tail lights, the instrument panel lighting and the luggage compartment light (10 amp fuse).

Fuse No. 2—The hanging lamp socket, the parking lights, the roof light and the horns (18 amp fuse).

Fuse No. 3—The indicator lights, the stoplights and the magnetic fan (10 amp fuse).

Fuse No. 4—The heater and the windscreen wiper (10 amp fuse).

The layout of the fuse box can be seen in **FIG 11:7**.

From 1968 a fuseboard containing 5 fuses is fitted. The fuse rating and the circuits they protect can be seen from the wiring diagrams (see Appendix).

11:6 Lights

The headlights, either Marchal, Ducellier or Cibié, are of the assymetric beam type. To adjust the headlights, special checking equipment must be used. The adjustment is made by removing the headlight rim and for the vertical adjustment on Marchal and Ducellier headlamps the upper adjusting screw is used and for the vertical adjustment on Cibie lamps the lower screw.

For the lateral adjustment on all lamps use either of the lateral adjusting screws.

The headlamps may be easily switched over for driving in either lefthand or righthand traffic. In order to reverse the assymetric beam, the notch guide lever of the bulb can be moved sideways (see **FIG 11:8**). Move the guide to the right for lefthand side traffic and to the left for righthand side traffic.

Side, indicator and brake lights:

At the front of the car the side lights and indicator lights are housed in one double filament bulb. The parking lights on both front wings act as indicator light repeaters when the parking light control is switched off.

At the rear of the car (see **FIG 11:9**), the top light is the indicator which has a yellow bulb. The centre light is the rear light and the bottom light the brake light, both of which are red.

The instrument panel lights are lit when the side or headlamps are switched on, thereby acting as a lighting indicator.

The roof light is controlled by a switch actuated when the front doors are opened. This control can be overridden by a separate switch inside the car.

11:7 Accessories:

The electrical clock is permanently fed direct from the battery. If at any time the battery has been switched off or disconnected the clock must be restarted.

The SEV windscreen wiper motor is installed under the bonnet (see **FIG 11:10**). It is controlled from a switch on the dashboard, and is of the self-parking type, switching off when the blades are in the bottom position. This leaves the windscreen unobstructed when in the off position.

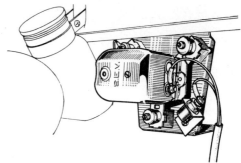

FIG 11:10 The windscreen wiper motor

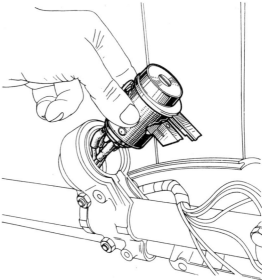

FIG 11:11 Fitting a Neiman Anti-theft switch

The horn control ring on the steering wheel will sound the horn when pressed at any point on its perimeter.

The Dauvauto main ignition switch, which is fitted into the housing on the steering column can be replaced by a Neiman antitheft switch (see **FIG 11:11**). The switch will come with the fitting instructions included and the electrical connections are as follows:

Wires 13 and 20 to positive terminal (20).

Wire 32 to Terminal B (15).

Wire 46 to Terminal D (50).

11:8 The alternator

From 1968 an alternator is fitted in place of the DC generator in the interests of securing a higher electrical output, particularly at low engine speeds.

There are a number of precautions to be observed when working on the alternator installation if serious trouble is to be avoided.

Check very carefully that any components fitted in the circuits are wired with the correct polarity as a wrong connection can cause irreparable damage in certain instances.

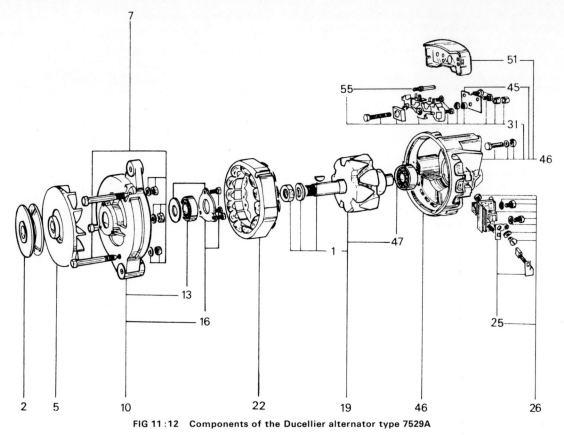

FIG 11:12 Components of the Ducellier alternator type 7529A

Key to Fig 11:12 1 Pulley drive   2 Pulley   5 Fan   7 Assembly bolts   10 Drive-end bracket   13 Bearing   16 Bearing mounting   19 Rotor assembly   22 Stator   25 Brushes   26 Brush carrier   31 Push-in terminal set   45 Fuse   46 Rear-end bracket   47 Rear bearing   51 Terminal cover   55 Diode carrier

Do not make or break any connections while the engine is running. Do not run the engine with the battery disconnected.

Always disconnect the battery before working on the alternator.

Do not start the engine when a charger or booster is still connected.

Disconnect the alternator when carrying out any welding on the car.

Two types of alternator are used: Ducellier type 7529A or Paris-Rhone A.13M3 with their respective regulator units 8362A or AYA21 (yellow).

Ducellier type 7529A (see FIG 11:12):

In the event of a fault in the charging circuit, first check the operation of the alternator in the car as follows:

Connect an ammeter in series in the output circuit (thick cable), then disconnect the excitation cable and with a separate wire connect the alternator excitation terminal to the battery + terminal.

Check the drive belt and run the alternator up to about 3500 rev/min and observe the reading on the ammeter. The output should show 22 amps approximately. If this reading is obtained it is the regulator that is at fault and should be renewed.

Checking the diodes:

As the diode carrier is removable this check can be carried out without breaking the soldered diode connections.

Connect a 12-volt test lamp rig across the diode terminals singly and in each direction. The lamp should light in one direction only. If it does not light at all or lights in both directions the diode is faulty and the assembly must be renewed.

Paris-Rhone type A.13M3:

This is an alternator of similar characteristics to that just described and may be checked for correct operation in a similar manner, except for the checking of the diodes which must be done using a battery ohmmeter which can measure the resistance of each diode in each direction.

Connect the polarised voltage source of the meter between the output end of the diode and the housing and then reverse the meter polarity. The following readings should be obtained:

Direct resistance   . .   30 ohms
Reverse resistance   . .   300,000 to 400,000 ohms

If direct resistance is zero, the diode is shortcircuited. If it is infinite the diode is burnt.

In view of the specialised equipment required for adequately servicing the alternator, the home operator is strongly advised to take a faulty instrument to a service station for attention or replacement.

11:9 Printed circuit instrument panel

This panel can be taken out as a complete assembly with all its instruments and bulbs.

First disconnect the battery, then take out the lower panels of the facia above the pedal mounting. Disconnect the speedometer cable and the trip control.

Take out the central butterfly screw and ease the complete panel out towards the front.

Disconnect the connector blocks on the left and right, and also the earthing cable.

The assembly may be dismantled after removing the rheostat knob and the clock setting button and releasing the 12 screws around the periphery of the panel.

Reassembly is a reversal of the above, being careful to replace correctly the speedometer trip control. It is advisable to check the operation of this before refitting the panel.

The various electric bulbs are held in plastic bayonet fittings and if required these may be removed and replaced after removing the lower panels of the facia above the pedal mounting, without disturbing the main panel.

11:10 Fault diagnosis

(a) Battery discharged

1 Terminals loose or dirty
2 Lighting circuit shorted
3 Generator not charging
4 Regulator or cut-out units not operating correctly
5 Battery internally defective

(b) Insufficient charging current

1 Loose or corroded battery terminals
2 Generator driving belt slipping

(c) Battery will not hold a charge

1 Low electrolyte level
2 Battery plates sulphated
3 Electrolyte leakage from cracked casing or top sealing compound
4 Plate separators ineffective

(d) Battery overcharged

1 Voltage regulator not controlling

(e) Generator output low or nil

1 Belt broken or slipping
2 Regulator unit not controlling correctly
3 Worn bearings, loose polepieces
4 Commutator worn, burnt or shorted
5 Armature shaft bent or worn
6 Insulation proud between commutator segments
7 Brushes sticking, springs weak or broken
8 Field coil wires shorted, broken or burned

(f) Starter motor lacks power or will not operate

1 Pinion sticking in mesh with flywheel
2 Battery discharged, loose cable connections
3 Starter switch faulty
4 Brushes worn or sticking, leads detached or shorting
5 Commutator dirty or worn
6 Starter shaft bent
7 Engine abnormally stiff
8 Armature or field coils faulty

(g) Starter motor runs but does not turn engine

1 Pinion sticking on screwed sleeve
2 Broken teeth on pinion or flywheel

(h) Noisy starter pinion when engine is running

1 Restraining spring weak or broken

(j) Starter motor rough or noisy

1 Mounting bolts loose
2 Damaged pinion or flywheel teeth
3 Main pinion spring broken

(k) Lamps inoperative or erratic

1 Battery low, bulbs burned out
2 Faulty earthing of lamps or battery
3 Lighting switch faulty, loose or broken wiring connections

(l) Wiper motor sluggish, taking high current

1 Faulty armature
2 Bearings out of alignment
3 Commutator dirty or short circuited

NOTES

CHAPTER 12

THE BODYWORK

12:1 Bodywork finish

The finish of the car may be kept in good condition by regular washing and polishing. First remove all excess mud and dirt by hosing the car down. Have two sets of sponges and chamois leathers, one set for the car panels and the other for the parts of the car which may remain a little greasy. After hosing the car, clean with the sponge and dry with the chamois leather which must be frequently rinsed out and wrung dry.

All polish products on the market may be safely used on the synthetic lacquer finish.

Windows and windscreens may be cleaned first by spraying or applying water liberally with a sponge, and then by drying with the chamois and finally polished with a clean dry cloth.

Large scale repairs to the body panels are best left to expert beaters. Even small dents can be tricky, as too much hammering will stretch the metal and make things worse instead of better. Filling in minor dents and scratches is probably the best method of restoring the surface. The touching up of paintwork is well within the powers of most car owners, particularly as self-spraying cans of paint in the correct colours are now usually available. It must be remembered however, that paint changes colour with age and it is better to spray a whole wing rather than try to touch up a small area.

Before spraying or painting it is essential to remove all traces of wax polish with white spirit. More drastic treatment is necessary if silicone polishes have been used. Use a primer surfacer or paste stopper according to the amount of filling required, and when it is dry, rub it down with 400 grade 'Wet or Dry' paper until the surface is smooth and flush with the surrounding area. Spend time on getting the best finish possible as this will control the final finish. Apply the retouching paint, keeping it wet in the centre and light and dry around the edges.

Allow to dry for a few hours and use a cutting compound to remove the dry spray around the edges of the refinished area. Finally, repolish with a liquid polish.

12:2 Removing and refitting the sunroof

1 Protect the front seats with covers and then close and lock the sunroof.
2 Remove the four front crossmember fixation screws.
3 Lift the crossmember, unscrew the nuts and locknuts from the lock rods (see **FIG 12:1**), and remove the roof.

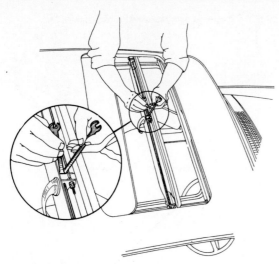

FIG 12:1 Roof removal. Releasing the locknuts from the lock rods

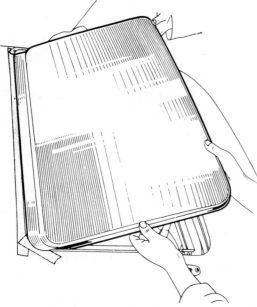

FIG 12:2 Refitting the sun roof

Refitting:

1 Install the crossmember, locks and the rods.
2 Tighten the nuts to obtain an equal tension between both rods and a normal stiffness in the operation of the handle. Carefully lock the locknuts. This operation can be done without removing the roof and should be performed whenever the handle fails to lock correctly.
3 Protect the rear of the roof with adhesive tape.
4 Engage the tension springs equipped with the upper rollers, under the roof.

5 Engage the panel (see **FIG 12:2**), so as to engage the lower slider rollers under the roof.
6 Position and fix the crossmember onto the panel.
7 Actuate the sunroof and check for correct operation. If when operating the sunroof it gets jammed sideways, close the roof and check the lower rollers for position on the sliders. Adjust the sliders so that the rollers start together up the slopes when the roof starts to move.

12:3 Door catch adjustments

1 Ensure that the latch and its control is operating correctly and that the door hinges are tight and not distorted.
2 Refer to **FIG 12:3** and loosen the three catch attachment screws and move the catch to its furthest outboard adjustment.
3 Press, without releasing, the outer handle knob and close the door slowly, pushing it hard in the closed position.
4 Open the door and release the control knob.
5 Tighten the catch attachment screws.
6 Check the door for correct closing and locking and recorrect as necessary.

The sole and the rod of the door catch should be oiled occasionally but do not put oil onto the nylon safety slope.

12:4 Removing and replacing the windscreen glass

Removal:

1 If the glass is being removed because it is cracked, stick adhesive tape or adhesive paper over the whole surface.
2 Ensure that the ventilator intake inlets and grilles are closed and the defroster slits are covered.
3 Remove the windscreen wiper arms.
4 Remove the sunvisor and the rear view mirror.

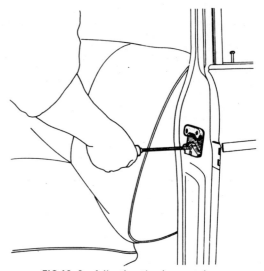

FIG 12:3 Adjusting the door catches

5 Remove the windscreen panel upright pilasters and the half circle trims.

6 Push off the windscreen and seal from the inside to the outside, if necessary striking with a rubber mallett. If the windscreen will still not move, cut off the joint outer lip and then remove the glass and joint (see **FIG 12:4**).

7 If the windscreen has been broken carefully clean the inside of the car and remove any broken glass from the heating and ventilation hoses and outlets.

Inspection:

If the glass is to be used again, clean off the old sealing compound. Check for chipped edges as these are a potential source of cracking of the glass.

Where the windscreen glass is removed in order to correct water leaks or for replacement due to breakage, it is important to check the windshield aperture for distortion or damage. For this purpose, the windscreen glass can be used as a template by mounting the glass in the aperture with the aid of short lengths of rubber cut from a discarded joint. Check that the spacing between the edges of the glass and the aperture flange is uniform and that the contour of the flange compares favourably with that of the glass. Care should be taken to avoid scratching the glass or chipping the edges when using the glass as a template.

Mark any areas of the aperture requiring correction. Reform the aperture and recheck with the glass.

Refitting:

1 Clean the windscreen frame ensuring that all traces of sealing are removed from the outer panel.

2 Apply sealing compound to a new seal and fit it to the glass with the joint at the top dead centre of the glass.

3 Refer to **FIG 12:5** and fit two strings between the lips of the seal with the ends crossed at the top and bottom centre of the glass. The strings will slide easily if they are rubbed in tallow or beeswax before fitting. Use two small pieces of pipe threaded onto the string to facilitate easier handling.

4 The operation of fitting the glass to the frame is made much easier if there are two operators, one on the inside of the car and one outside. Position the glass on the frame with the string inside the car.

5 Pull alternately on each string to pull the inner lip over the inner panel.

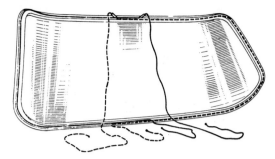

FIG 12:5   Preparation of windscreen for fitting

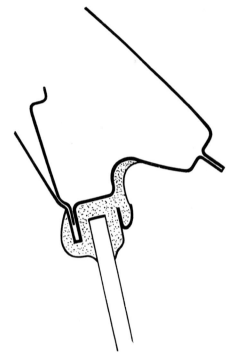

FIG 12:6   Section of the rear window and seal

6 At the same time push or strike gently from the outside of the glass until the seal is completely fitted over the inner panel.

7 Apply sealing compound between the outer lip of the seal and the outer panel.

8 Refit the windscreen wiper arms, the sun visor and the rear view mirror.

9 Refit the windscreen panel upright pilasters and the half circle trims.

12:5 Removing and replacing the rear window

Removal:

Remove the rear seat and the seat back and proceed in the same manner as for the removal of the windscreen.

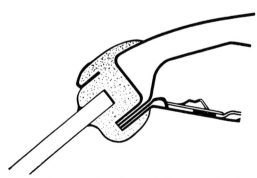

FIG 12:4   Section of the windscreen and seal

FIG 12:7 The door of the Cabriolet

Key to Fig 12:7   1 Upholstery attaching screws
2 Lower trim bar attaching screws

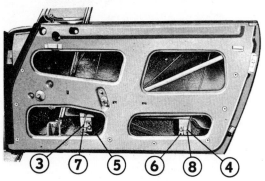

12:8 Door with upholstery removed

Key to Fig 12:8   3/4 Window attachment points
5/6 Window stops   7/8 Cable clamps

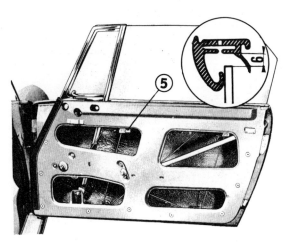

FIG 12:9 Adjustment of window upper stop

Key to Fig 12:9   5 Front stop

Refitting:

The fitting of the rear window is the same as that for the windscreen but it is only necessary to use one string. A section of the glass and seal can be seen in **FIG 12:6**.

12:6 Replacing door window of 404 Cabriolet
Removing the window:

1 Refer to **FIG 12:7** and remove the window lifter crank and the inner door-opening handle.
2 Remove the two screws 1, located under the arm rest. The arm rest remains attached to the upholstery panel.
3 Remove both attachment screws 2, for the lower trim bar.
4 Unstitch the upholstery panel and pull it down to remove it.
5 Remove the upper trim strip which is located by three screws. Slide it rearwards to disengage it from the ventilator handle.
6 Pull off the vinyl sheet which covers the inner door panel.
7 Mark the glass panel fitting attachment points on both sections of the cable (see items 3 and 4 of **FIG 12:8**).
8 Remove both glass panel stops, items 5 and 6, and both cable clamps, items 7 and 8, and remove the glass panel.
9 If the glass has been broken remove all glass from the lower part of the door.

Preparation of new glass:

Clean the glass panel fitting thoroughly to remove all traces of sealing compound.

Smear the new rubber wedge and the fitting with cement and place them on the new glass panel. The distance between the end of the fitting and the front end of the glass panel should be 72 mm. Remove any excess cement.

Refitting the window glass:

1 Check the alignment of the ventilator in relation to the slide on the door. The ventilator should be removed and straightened if it is bent.
2 Engage the glass panel in the slide, making sure that it does not bind, and lower it fully. Adjust the position of the rear slide if necessary.
3 Assemble the cable clamps and insert the cable between the plates of the clamps. Bring the reference marks into alignment and tighten the cable clamp screws.
4 To adjust the upper stop, close the door and raise the window until its top edge is 6 mm from the bottom of the upper rubber gasket (see **FIG 12:9**).
5 Install the front stop (see item 5 of **FIG 12:9**), against the corresponding pad on the door inner panel and tighten the attachment screw.
6 To adjust the lower stop, lower the window until the top of the glass is flush with the outer trim and rubber gasket.
7 Install the rear stop against the corresponding pad on the door inner panel and tighten the attachment screw.
8 Check that the glass panel slides freely and leave it in the up position.

9 Cement the vinyl sheet onto the door inner panel.
10 Refit the trim strip, the upholstery panel and the door
opening handle.
11 Install the window lifter handle by turning it towards
the front and slanting it approximately 45 deg. downwards.

12:7 Replacing window lifter and cable assembly, 404 Cabriolet

1 Remove the glass panel as detailed in **Section 12:6.**
2 Remove the window lifter.
3 Slacken the cable tensioner (see inset to **FIG 12:10**),
located on the lower pulley bar. To gain access to the
tensioner screw, remove the rubber plug from the
bottom of the door. Remove the cable.
4 Check that all four pulleys rotate freely (see item 2 of
FIG 12:10).
5 Fit the new window lifter and engage the cable on the
four pulleys in succession as shown in **FIG 12:10**.
The section of the cable, item 4, should be in front of
the other cable sections.
6 Turn the tensioner screw as required to obtain
moderate tension on the cable.
7 Adjust the position of the lower pulley bar by
slackening the attachment screws, item 3, to prevent
the cable runs from rubbing against each other.
8 Insert the glass panel in the slides and check that the
panel does not bind, then lower it fully.
9 Turn the window lifter crank fully back, and then
rotate it forward by two turns.
10 Install both cable clamps with the crank in this
position, and tighten the cable clamp screws.
11 Install and adjust the window stops as detailed in
Section 12:6.
12 Check for correct operation and lubricate the window
lifter mechanism.
13 Raise the window and install the trim strip, upholstery
panel, door opening handle and window lifter crank.
This should be turned towards the front and slanted
45 deg. downwards.

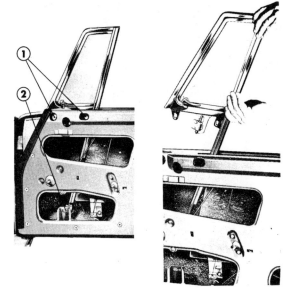

FIG 12:11   Details of door ventilator

Key to Fig 12:11   1 Upper attachment screws
2 Lower attachment nut

FIG 12:12   Ventilator adjustment

Key to Fig 12:12   3 Outer edge of rubber gasket
4 Inner edge of rubber gasket

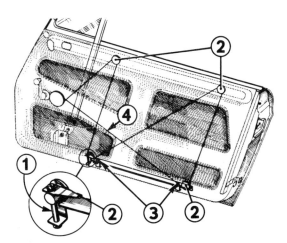

FIG 12:10   Details of cable assembly for window lift

Key to Fig 12:10   1 Cable tensioner   2 Pulleys   3 Lower
pulley bar screws   4 Cable

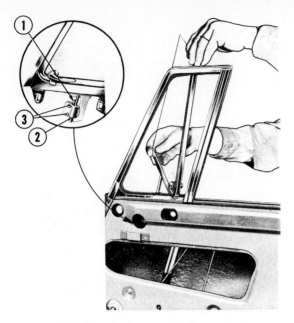

FIG 12:13 Ventilator mobile frame details

Key to Fig 12:13 1/2 Stop screws on lower pivot rod
3 Friction device adjusting screws

12:8 Removing and refitting a ventilator, 404 Cabriolet

Removal:

1 Remove the upholstery panel and the trim strip as detailed in **Section 12:6.**
2 Refer to **FIG 12:11** and remove both upper attachment screws 1, and the lower attachment nut 2.
3 Lift the ventilator to remove from the door.

Refitting:

1 Fit the ventilator to the door and engage the upper and lower attachments but do not tighten at this stage.
2 Adjust the ventilator by moving the lower attachment screw in its slot to obtain an even clearance of 5 mm between the ventilator frame and the windscreen lateral upright (see **FIG 12:12**).
3 Move the lower attachment laterally to bring the the ventilator in complete contact with the door rubber gasket and to get the correct angle of the glass panel. The outside lip of the rubber gasket (see item 3 of **FIG 12:2**), should cover the glass panel, and the glass panel should bear against the inner lip, item 4.
4 Tighten the ventilator attachment screws and nut.
5 Check that the window glass slides freely and adjust the lower attachment of the window rear channel if necessary.
6 Re-install the trim strip, upholstery panel, door opening handle and the window lifter as detailed in **Section 12:6.**

12:9 Replacing the mobile frame of ventilator, 404 Cabriolet

Removal:

1 Remove the upholstery panel and the trim strip (see **Section 12:6**).
2 Refer to **FIG 12:13** and remove both stop screws, items 1 and 2, on the lower pivot rod.
3 Remove the upper pivot screw.
4 Slacken both screws, item 3, on the lower bearing.
5 Lift the mobile frame and turn it inwards to remove it.

FIG 12:14 Folding top attachments and correct stowage

Key to Fig 12:14 1 Snap fasteners 2 Velco strip
3 Top rim attachment screws

Refitting:

Refitting the mobile frame is the exact reverse of the removal instructions. The rotational friction of the ventilator can be adjusted by tightening or slackening the screws (see item 3 of **FIG 12:13**).

12:10 Lowering procedure for folding top on convertible

1 Unlock both left- and righthand top attachments at the upper part of the windscreen pillars, by pulling the locking handles until the striker is released.
2 Open the rear window by sliding the zip fastener runner across the top to the opposite side until it is completely undone.
3 Refer to **FIG 12:14** and release both left- and righthand side snap fasteners, item 1, and unfasten the rear window and the folding top on each side.
4 Clear the rear of the top storage recess by unfastening the Velco strip, item 2.
5 Slacken all five attachment screws, item 3, of the rear top rim and remove the window assembly.
6 Install the rear top rim and the rear plastic window flat against the bottom of the top storage recess. Do not fold the transparent panel.
7 Unlatch the stretching links of the top rear bail by pulling the button upwards.
8 Fold back the top and arrange neatly in its recess. Ensure that the cloth does not get caught up in the metal fittings or the edges of the body.
9 Raising the folding top is the exact reversal of the lowering procedure.

12:11 Heating and ventilation

The roof is one of the best ventilation means the 404 owner has. It can be fully opened at high speeds with no draught to bother front seat passengers at all. This is even possible in winter due to a heater unit which is very efficient. In very cold conditions the heater can be used as a recirculating heater and on milder days it can be used as a fresh air unit. The air intake is under the windscreen where it draws in pure air rather than exhaust fumes. Air vents are fitted at each side of the facia panel so that each front seat occupant can control his own supply of fresh air. These are completely separate from the central heater-ventilator system and a type of replacement for side window ventilators.

The heater unit is a Sofica Climatizer and allows all combinations of heating, demisting, defrosting and ventilation. The unit which consists of a bakelite casing containing a radiator and an electrical motor and turbine, can be seen in section in **FIG 12:15**. This diagram also shows the air flow through the unit for different shutter positions.

12:12 Seat belts

As from Serial No. 404.4.444.551 the front floor has been reinforced and incorporates 4 tapped anchor points for securing safety belts (see **FIG 12:16**).

It is dangerous to fit seat belts incorrectly. If an owner feels that his skill and equipment may not enable him to make a safe installation, he is strongly advised to entrust the work to an Authorized Dealer.

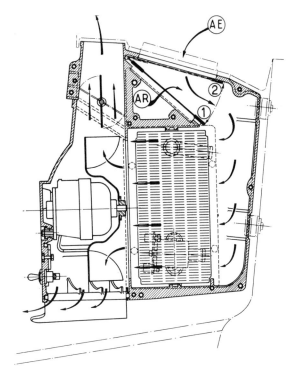

FIG 12:15   The Sofica Climatizer

Key to Fig 12:15   **AE** External air intake, shutter in
position 1   **AR** Recirculated air, shutter in position 2

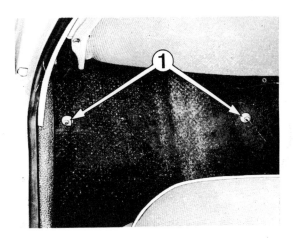

FIG 12:16   Seat belt anchorages

On cars not already fitted with anchorage points, the fitting of seat belts involves welding reinforcement plates to the floor and these plates can be ordered by your Peugeot Agent.

APPENDIX

TECHNICAL DATA

Engine   Fuel system   Ignition system   Cooling system
Clutch   Gearbox   Rear axle   Front suspension
Rear suspension   Steering   Wheels and tyres
Brakes   Electrical equipment   Torque wrench settings

WIRING DIAGRAMS AND SPECIAL TOOLS

FIG 13:1   Wiring diagram, saloon and estate cars
FIG 13:2   Wiring diagram, coupé 1968
FIG 13:3   Wiring diagram, saloon 1970
FIG 13:4   Wiring diagram of the Jaeger Coupler
FIG 13:5   Timing adjustment check rod

HINTS ON MAINTENANCE AND OVERHAUL

GLOSSARY OF TERMS

INDEX

TECHNICAL DATA

Dimensions are in inches unless otherwise stated

ENGINE

General:

Engine type	XC
Number of cylinders	4
Bore...	84 mm (3.307 inches)
Stroke	73 mm (2.874 inches)
Capacity	1618 cc
Compression ratio	7.2:1, 7.4:1 or 7.6:1
Maximum bhp	66 at 5400 rev/min
Maximum rev/min	5400
Maximum torque	94 lb ft at 2250 rev/min
Cylinder liners	Removable wet type

Valves:

Head diameter:	Inlet	1.535
	Exhaust	1.319
Stem diameter:	Inlet	.335
	Exhaust	.334
Overall length:	Inlet	4.7
	Exhaust	4.4
Face angle:	Inlet	30 deg.
	Exhaust	45 deg.

Valve timing:

Inlet opens	0 deg. TDC
Inlet closes	30 deg. 30' ABDC
Exhaust opens	30 deg. BBDC
Exhaust closes	4 deg. 30' ATDC
Rocker clearance for valve timing	.0275

Valve springs:

Free length:	Inner	1.685
	Outer	1.850
Inner diameter:	Inner	.554
	Outer	.842
Number of active coils:	Inner	7
	Outer	$4\frac{3}{4}$
Wire diameter	Inner	.110
	Outer	.149
Length under load:	Inner	1.170 inch at 49 lb
	Outer	1.326 inch at 81 lb

Valve guides and seat inserts:

Guide outside diameter:

	Cylinder head bore	
Standard	.550	.552
1st oversize	.5626	.5591
2nd oversize	.5744	.5709

Inlet seat inserts diameter:

Standard	1.5811	1.5748
1st oversize	1.5889	1.5826
2nd oversize	1.6008	1.5945

Exhaust seat inserts diameter:

Standard	1.383	1.3779
1st oversize	1.3909	1.3858
2nd oversize	1.4027	1.3976

Cylinder liners and pistons:

Cylinder bore diameter:

Grade I	3.3071 to 3.3075

Grade II	3.30755 to 3.30795
Grade III	3.30799 to 3.30837
Grade IV	3.3084 to 3.3088

Piston diameters:

Grade A	3.3047 to 3.3051
Grade B	3.3051 to 3.3056
Grade C	3.3056 to 3.3060
Grade D	3.3060 to 3.3064

Cylinder liner grading marks are ground on the lower edge of the liners on the camshaft side of the engine when the liners are installed. Piston grading letters are stamped on the crown of the piston and correspond respectively to the cylinder liner grading marks according to size. Piston skirt is measured at 90 deg. to the gudgeon pin axis.

Maximum weight variation in any two pistons of an engine	8 to 10 grammes
Number of ring grooves	3
Ring groove width: Top	.0795
Second	.0787
Oil control	.1772
Gudgeon pin bore diameter	.866
Gudgeon pin bore offset in piston	.037

Piston rings:

Number of compression rings	2
Number of oil control rings	1
Width of compression rings	.078
Width of oil control ring	.1764
Ring gap (fitted)	.0155
Ring to groove clearance: Compression	.0015
Oil control	.0008

Gudgeon pins:

Gudgeon pin diameter:

Standard	.8663
1st oversize	.8681
2nd oversize	.870
Gudgeon pin length	2.756
Gudgeon pin fit in piston	.0003 inch interference

Connecting rods:

Length between centres	5.197
Big-end width	1.178
Big-end bore diameter	2.113
Small-end width	.866
Small-end bore diameter without bush	.945

Connecting rod weight identification symbols:	1 ...	591 to 610 grammes
	2 ...	611 to 630 grammes
	3 ...	631 ro 650 grammes
	4 ...	651 to 670 grammes
	5 ...	671 to 690 grammes
	6 ...	691 to 710 grammes

These weight symbols apply to complete connecting rods without bearing shells, and are etched on the side of the rods opposite to the camshaft when assembled in the engine.

Crankshaft:

Main bearing journal diameter:	Front	2.339
	Centre	2.306
	Rear	2.015
Main bearing journal length:	Front	1.496
	Centre	1.496
	Rear	1.457
Crankpin diameter		1.9685

Crankpin length	...	...	...	...	1.181
Crankshaft end float	...	...	...	...	.003 to .008
End thrust taken	...	...	...	...	Rear main bearing

Thrust washer sizes:

Standard	...	...	...	...	.0905
1st oversize ...	...	...	...	...	.0945
2nd oversize	...	...	...	...	.0965
3rd oversize ...	...	...	...	...	.0984

Main bearing journal undersizes:

Front:	1st undersize	...	...	...	...	2.327
	2nd undersize	...	...	...	...	2.319
	3rd undersize	...	...	...	...	2.307
Centre:	1st undersize	...	...	...	...	2.294
	2nd undersize	...	...	...	...	2.286
	3rd undersize	...	...	...	...	2.254
Rear:	1st undersize	...	...	...	...	2.003
	2nd undersize	...	...	...	...	1.995
	3rd undersize	...	...	...	...	1.983

Crankpin undersizes:

1st undersize	...	...	...	...	1.956
2nd undersize	...	...	...	...	1.948
3rd undersize	...	...	...	...	1.936

Main and big-end bearings:

Main bearing half shell thickness:

Standard ...	...	...	...	...	.0745 to .0748
1st undersize	...	...	...	...	.0805 to .0807
2nd undersize	...	...	...	...	.0844 to .0846
3rd undersize	...	...	...	...	.0903 to .0905

Big-end bearing half shell thickness:

Standard	...	...	...	...	.0716 to .0718
1st undersize	...	...	...	...	.0775 to .0777
2nd undersize	...	...	...	...	.0814 to .0817
3rd undersize	...	...	...	...	.0873 to .0876

Camshaft bearings and tappets:

Camshaft bearing inside diameter:

Front	...	...	...	...	1.889
Centre	...	...	...	...	1.811
Rear	...	...	...	...	1.732

Camshaft bearing length:

Front	...	...	...	...	.965
Centre	...	...	...	...	.7874
Rear	...	...	...	...	1.240

Tappet diameter

Standard ...	...	...	...	...	.945
Oversize ...	...	...	...	...	.953
Tappet length	...	...	...	...	1.496

Timing chain and tensioner:

Type of chain	...	...	...	...	Duplex roller
Number of pitches ...	...	...	...	...	58
Crankshaft gear teeth	...	...	...	...	19
Camshaft gear teeth...	...	...	...	...	38
Type of chain tensioner	...	...	...	...	Renolds
Free length of tensioner spring	...	...	...	2.914
Tensioner spring length under load ...	...	...	1.968 inches at 3.6 lb
Tensioner oil inlet orifice diameter ...	...	...	.0315
Tensioner oil outlet orifice diameter...	...	...	.040

Pushrods and rockers:

Pushrod length:

Inlet	...	...	...	...	...	7.125
Exhaust	...	...	...	...	...	8.464
Rocker shaft length		...	...	...	...	17.4

Valve stem to rocker clearance—cold:

Inlet	...	...	...	...	...	.004
Exhaust	...	...	...	...	...	.010

Later engines:

Compression ratio	XC5	...	...	...	...	7.6:1
	XC6	...	...	...	...	8.3:1
	XC7	...	...	...	...	7.6:1
Max. bhp (SAE)	XC5	...	...	...	...	76 at 5500 rev/min
	XC6	...	...	...	...	80 at 5600 rev/min
	XC7	...	...	...	...	73 at 5600 rev/min

Valves:

Head diameter:	Inlet	...	...	...	...	1.633
	Exhaust	...	...	...	...	1.397
Stem diameter:	Inlet	...	...	...	...	.3156
	Exhaust	...	...	...	...	.3149
Length:	Inlet	...	...	...	...	4.671
	Exhaust	...	...	...	...	4.409

Crankshaft:

Main bearing journal diameter:	Front	...	...	2.339
	Front intermediate	...		2.3059
	Centre	...	...	2.2516
	Rear intermediate	...		2.2114
	Rear	...	...	2.015

Lubrication:

Type of pump	...	...	...	...	...	Geared
Type of filter	...	...	...	...	...	Replaceable element
Pressure relief valve position		...	...	...		In pump cover
Pressure relief valve operates		...	...	...		99 lb/sq inch
Oil pressure warning light operates	...		...	...		Below 10 lb/sq inch
Oil filter capacity	...	...	...	...	...	Approx. 1 pint
Oil sump capacity	...	...	...	...	...	7 pints
Oil grade	...	...	...	...	...	SAE.20W/30 or 40
Oil change frequency		...	...	...	...	Every 3000 miles

FUEL SYSTEM

Carburetter type (XC and early XC5 engines)	...		...	Solex 32 PBICA or Zenith 34 WIM
Carburetter type (late XC5 engines)	...	...	...	Solex 34 PBICA

Specifications—Solex 32 PBICA:

Choke tube	...	...	...	...	...	25
Main jet	...	...	...	...	...	130
Correction jet	...	...	...	...	...	170
Pilot jet (petrol)	...	...	...	...	...	50
Pilot jet (air), under choke tube		...	...	...	220
Pilot jet (air) on mating surface		...	...	...	0
Starter jet (petrol)	...	...	...	...	...	110
Starter jet (air)	...	...	...	...	...	6.5
Emulsion tube	...	...	...	...	...	19
Accelerating pump jet	...	...	...	...	45
Accelerating pump injector	...	...	...	...	50
Float	...	...	...	...	...	5.7g
Needle valve	...	...	...	...	...	1.7
Carburetter flange gasket Part No.	...	...	...	0366.04
Gasket inside diameter	...	...	...	...	33 mm

Specifications—Solex 34 PBICA:

Choke tube	...	...	...	...	...	26

Main jet	...	...	...	...	...	137
Correction jet	...	...	...	...	...	170
Pilot jet (petrol)	...	...	...	...	...	45
Pilot jet (air) under choke tube		...	...	...	...	210
Pilot jet (air) on mating surface		...	...	...	...	0
Starter jet (petrol)	...	...	...	...	...	110
Starter jet (air)	...	...	...	...	...	6.5
Emulsion tube	...	...	...	...	...	28
Accelerating pump jet	...	...	...	...	45
Accelerating pump injector	...	...	...	...	50
Float	...	...	...	...	...	5.7g
Needle valve	...	...	...	...	...	1.7
Carburetter flange gasket Part No.	...	...	...	...	1406.34
Gasket internal diameter	...	...	...	...	35 mm

Specifications—Zenith 34 WIM:

Choke tube	...	...	...	...	...	26
Main jet	...	...	...	...	...	135
Correction jet	...	...	...	...	...	100
Slow-running jet	...	...	...	...	...	65
Slow-running air vent	...	...	...	...	150
Float level (from the joint face)		...	...	...	17 to 18 mm
Fuel pump type	...	...	...	...	...	Mechanical

IGNITION SYSTEM

Distributor:

Make	...	...	...	...	...	Ducellier, SEV, or Paris-Rhone
Control	...	...	...	...	...	Centrifugal and vacuum advance
Ignition advance	...	...	...	...	...	11 deg. on flywheel
Contact breaker point gap	...	...	...	...	.020 inch
Cam angle	...	...	...	...	...	57 deg.

Sparking plugs:

XC engine	...	...	...	...	...	Marchal 36 P, AC 44F
XC 5, 7 engines	...	...	...	...	...	Marchal 36 HS, AC P44XL
XC 6 engine	...	...	...	...	...	Marchal 35 HS, AC 44XL
Spark gap	...	...	...	...	...	.024 inch
Firing order	...	...	...	...	...	1-3-4-2

COOLING SYSTEM

Capacity	...	...	...	...	...	14 pints
Fan type	...	...	...	...	...	Magnetic clutch
Fan drive engages at	...	...	...	...	185°F
Fan drive disengages at	...	...	...	...	167°F
Fan operation	...	...	...	...	...	Thermo-switch

CLUTCH

Make	...	...	...	...	...	Ferodo, dry plate
Type	...	...	...	...	...	PKSC
Pressure plate springs, number		...	...	...	9
Thrust bearing type	...	...	...	...	Carbon graphite
Type	...	...	...	...	...	215D
Pressure plate spring	...	...	...	...	Diaphragm
Thrust bearing type	...	...	...	...	Ball race
Outside diameter of linings	...	...	...	...	8.46
Inside diameter of linings	...	...	...	...	5.7

GEARBOX

Type	C3
Gear ratios (gearbox with letter A prefix):	
1st gear	4.08:1
2nd gear	2.21:1
3rd gear	1.42:1
Top	1.00:1
Reverse	4.40:1
Gear ratios (gearbox with letter B prefix):	
1st gear	4.00:1
2nd gear	2.24:1
3rd gear	1.44:1
Top	1.00:1
Reverse	4.33:1
Gearbox oil capacity	$2\frac{1}{4}$ pints
Type	BA7
Gear ratios:	
1st gear	3.663:1
2nd gear	2.169:1
3rd gear	1.409:1
Top	1:1
Reverse	3.747:1
Oil capacity	2.6 pints
Oil grade	SAE.20W/30 or 40
Oil change	Every 6000 miles

REAR AXLE

Rear axle drive...	Torque tube and universal joint
Rear axle type	Worm and wheel or hypoid bevel
Ratios:	
Worm type	4 × 19 or 5 × 21
Bevel type	8 × 37 or 9 × 38
Oil capacity	2.5 pints
Oil type	Essolube VT

FRONT SUSPENSION

Type	Lower wishbone connected to coil spring through shock absorber unit
Coil spring identification:	
1st type	1 red paint dash
2nd type	1 white paint dash
Spring height under load:	
1st type	7.165 to 7.362 inches at 701 lb
2nd type	7.362 to 7.56 inches at 701 lb
Camber angle	0 deg. 30′ ± 45′
Castor angle	2 deg. ± 1 deg.
Wheel alignment	2 mm ± 1 mm
Kingpin inclination	9 deg. 50′—10′

REAR SUSPENSION

Type	Coil spring and stabilizer bar
Coil spring identification:	
1st type	1. Single blue paint dash
	2. Single yellow paint dash
2nd type	1. Single green paint dash
	2. Two green paint dashes

Spring height under load:
1st type ... ...   1. 9.65 to 9.85 inches at 695 lb
                                                   2. 9.85 to 9.94 inches at 695 lb
2nd type ... ...   1. 9.45 to 9.65 inches at 695 lb
                                                   2. 6.65 to 9.85 inches at 695 lb

STEERING GEAR

Type ... ...   Rack and pinion

Early application to Engine No. 4025422:

Number of rack teeth   25
Number of pinion teeth   6
Ratio 20:1
Turning radius ... ...   15 ft 9$\frac{3}{4}$ inches
Steering wheel turns, lock to lock   4

Later application from Engine No. 4025423:

Number of rack teeth   30
Number of pinion teeth   8
Ratio 18.6:1
Turning radius ... ...   15 ft 9$\frac{3}{4}$ inches
Steering wheel turns, lock to lock 3.75

WHEELS AND TYRES

Tyre size ... ...   165 x 380
Rim size ... ...   155 x 380
Attachment holes   3
Wheel nut torque ... ...   43.3 lb ft
Tyre pressures:

Michelin SDS, Dunlop DS Front ... ...   20 lb/sq inch
  Kleber Colombes S75 Rear ... ...   23 lb/sq inch
  Michelin X Front ... ...   20 lb/sq inch·
                          Rear ... ...   23 lb/sq inch
  Dunlop S Front ... ...   25 lb/sq inch
                          Rear ... ...   29 lb/sq inch
  Kleber Colombes Front ... ...   23 lb/sq inch
                          Rear ... ...   25 lb/sq inch

BRAKING SYSTEM

Type of brake units:

Front ... ...   Bendix, two leading shoe or disc
Rear ... ...   Bendix, leading and trailing shoe
Operation ... ...   Lockheed hydraulic system
Handbrake ... ...   Cable on rear wheels
Lining type ... ...   Ferodo 4Z
Servo type ... ...   Hydrovac

Front wheel brake cylinders:

From Serial No. 4388566 ... ...   2 cylinders, 1$\frac{1}{8}$ inches diameter
From Serial No. 4012424 to ... ...   Front cylinder, 1$\frac{1}{8}$ inches diameter
        4108664 ... ...   Rear cylinder, 1$\frac{1}{4}$ inches diameter
From Serial No. 4108665 to 4388565 ... ...   2 cylinders, 30 mm diameter
From Serial No. 5100001 ... ...   2 cylinders, 1$\frac{3}{8}$ inches diameter

Rear wheel brake cylinders:

From beginning of series ... ...   1 cylinder, 1 inch diameter
From Serial No. 5100582 ... ...   1 cylinder, .629 inch diameter

ELECTRICAL EQUIPMENT

Battery:
- Type ... ... Lead/acid
- Voltage 12
- Specific gravity charged 1.290

Generator:
- Make ... ... Ducellier or Paris-Rhone
- Type:
  - Ducellier ... ... 72-10A or G
  - Paris-Rhone ... ... G11R—110
- Normal output ... ... 23 amp
  - Cut-in speed ... ... 1240 to 1280 rev/min
  - Field resistance ... ... 6.5 to 7.5 ohm
- Regulator type:
  - Ducellier 8297-16A
  - Paris-Rhone ... ... ID21—16D

Alternator:
- Type ... ... Ducellier 7529A
- Output ... ... 370 watts
- Current max. ... ... 27 amps
- Drive ratio 1.8:1
- Voltage 14
- Type ... ... Paris-Rhone A13M3
- Output ... ... 25 amps
- Cut-in speed ... ... 1000 rev/min 14 volts (warm)
- Brush minimum length ... ... 3 mm

Starter:
- Make ... ... Ducellier or Paris-Rhone
- Type:
  - Ducellier 6081
  - Paris-Rhone D8E-31
  - Torque at 3100 rev/min ... ... 3.61 lb ft
  - Lock torque ... ... 7.2 lb ft
  - Current consumption ... ... 260 amps
  - Rev/min free rotation 7500
  - Number of drive pinion teeth 9

TORQUE WRENCH SETTINGS
Dimensions are in lb ft unless otherwise stated

Engine:

Cylinder head screws	29, then 51
Rocker arm shaft on cylinder head	10.8 to 18
Connecting rod bolts	30.7 to 34.3
Crankshaft counterweight screws	43.3 to 47
Main bearing cap screws	50.6 to 57.8
Flywheel screws	43.7 to 47
Starting handle dog screws	72 to 87
Spark plugs	18 to 19.9
Engine front mount support	21.6 to 25.3
Engine rear support screws	21.6 to 25.3
Engine front stake (checker) screw	14.5 to 18
Engine support to front crossmember screw ...	36.1 to 43.3

Steering gear:

Steering rack control pinion	28.9 to 32.5
Steering gear to crossmember fixation	21.6 to 32.5
Flector attachment bolt	5.4 to 9

Brakes:

Brake plate screws	39.7 to 47
Brake line couplings	36.1 to 43.3
Bleeding screws	9.4 to 10.8

Front axle suspension:

Connecting rod bolt	36.1 to 50.6
Connecting ball head	36.1 to 39.7
Front hubs bearing nut	7.23 maximum
Front wishbone arms assembling nut	21.6 to 28.9
Wishbone front arm to rear arm axle attachment ...	21.6 to 28.9
Front wishbone rear arm to crossmember axle attachment	59.8 to 65
Ball head casing to rack (steering gear side) ...	28.9 to 36.1
Stub axle ball head nut	28.9 to 36.1
Front shock absorber closing nut	39.7 to 50.6
Front shock absorber rod upper nut	36.1 to 43.3
Front crossmember to bodyshell bolt	28.9 to 43.3

Rear axle:

Differential shell bolts:	Diameter 11 x 125 mm ...	43.7 to 54
	Diameter 10 x 125 mm ...	39.7 to 43.3
Stabilizer bar to yoke bolt		36.1 to 43.3
Stabilizer bar to bodyshell bolt		36.1 to 50.6

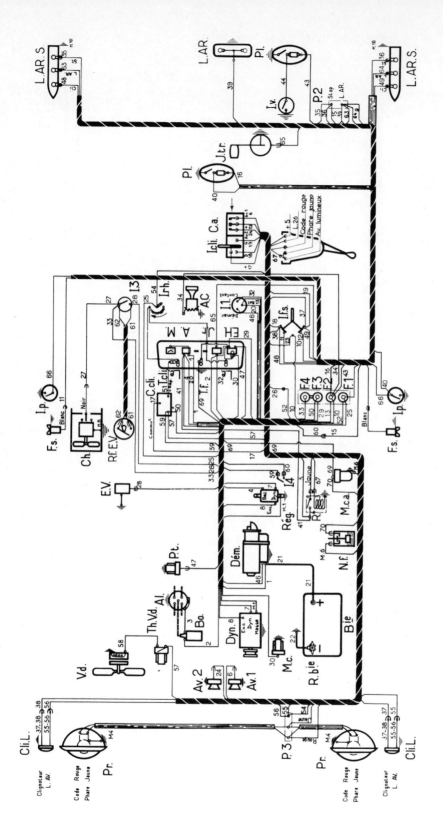

FIG 13:1 Wiring diagram of Saloon and Estate cars

Key to Fig 13:1 **A** Ammeter **AC** Cigar lighter **AI** Distributor and condenser **Av1** Town horn **Av2** Country horn **Bie** Battery **Bo** Ignition coil **Ca** Horn switch **Ccli** Flasher unit **Ch** Heating and air-conditioning equipment **CliL** Front flasher lamp and parking light **Com** Lighting switch **Dem** Starter, solenoid type **Dyn** Dynamo **EH** Water thermometer and oil pressure warm. lt **EV** Windscreen wiper **F1** Fuse, 18 amp. front and rear parking lights and facia board light **F2** Fuse, 18 amp. roof light sidelights, cigar lighter and horns **F3** Fuse, 10 amp. stoplights, flashers, and self-disengaging fan **F4** Fuse, 18 amp. air-conditioner and windscreen wiper **Fs** Sidelight **I1** Ignition and starter control switch (or Neiman anti-theft lock) **I3** Windscreen wiper switch and windscreen washer control assy **I4** Stoplight switch **Icli** Flasher selector switch **Ifs** Sidelight selector switch **Ip** Door switch **Irh** Facia board lighting rheostat and switch **Iv** Back gate switch **Jr** Fuel gauge indicator **Jtr** Fuel gauge transmitter **LAR** Rear lamp, license plate lighting **LARS** Rear parking light, stoplight, flasher **Le** Facia board light **M** Clock **Mc** Pressure switch, oil pressure warning light **Mca** Pressure switch, power brake system **Nf** Brake fluid level switch ('Nivocode') **P2** Plate, 2 terminals **P3** Plate, 3 terminals **Pl** Roof light and switch **Pr** Headlight **Pr** Windscreen wiper 'Relefix' parking switch **Pt** Socket, water thermometer **R** Signalling light relay **Rbie** Main battery switch **Reg** Voltage regulator and cut-out **Rf-ev** Windscreen wiper 'Relefix' parking switch **Tcli** Flashing indicator control light **Tf** Brake system warning light **ThVd** Self-disengaging fan thermal switch **Vd** Self-disengaging fan

122

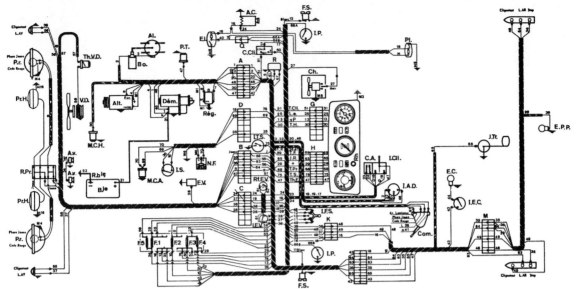

FIG 13:2   Wiring diagram Coupé 1968

Key to Fig 13:2   A to Q Connectors   **Alt** Alternator   **AC** Cigar lighter   **A1** Distributor   **Av** Horn   **Bie** Battery   **Bo** Ignition coil   **C.CR** Direction indicator switch   **Ch** Heater   **Com** Lighting switch   **Dem** Starter   **E.C.** Boot lamp   **E.P.P.** Rear number plate lamp   **E.V.** Windscreen wiper   **F.1, F.2, F.4, F.5** 15 Amp fuses   **F.3** 8 Amp fuse   **F.S.** Parking lamp   **H.E.** Oil pressure and water temperature indicator   **I.A.D.** Starter switch   **I. Cli.** Flasher switch   **I.E.C.** Boot lamp switch   **I.E.V.** Windscreen wiper switch   **I.F.S.** Parking lamp switch   **I.P.** Door switch   **I.S.** Stop lamp switch   **J.R.** Fuel gauge   **J. Tr.** Fuel tank unit   **L.Ar.** Rear lamps   **L.Av.** Side lamps   **L.E.** Panel lamp   **M.C.A.** Brake warning light   **N.F.** Brake fluid level warning   **P.E.** Petrol pump   **Pr.** Headlamp   **Pr.H.** Spot lamp   **P.T.** Water temperature sender unit   **R** Horn relay   **R.bie** Battery master switch   **Reg** Regulator   **Rf.E.V.** Windscreen wash relay   **Rh.** Rheostat   **R.Pr.** Headlamp relay   **T.Cli** Flasher warning lamp   **T.H.** Oil pressure warning lamp   **Th.E.** Water thermometer   **Th.V.D.** Fan switch   **T.P.R.** Headlamp warning light   **Th.T.** Water temperature warning lamp   **V.D.** Electro-magnetic fan

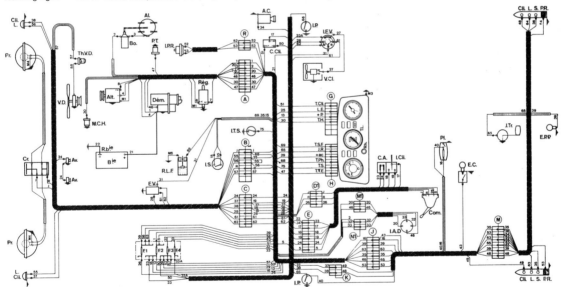

FIG 13:3   Wiring diagram Saloon 1970

Key to Fig 13:3   A to Q Connectors   **Alt** Alternator   **AC** Cigar lighter   **A1** Distributor   **Av** Horn   **Bie** Battery   **Bo** Ignition coil   **C.CR** Direction indicator switch   **Ch** Heater   **Com** Lighting switch   **Dem** Starter   **E.C.** Boot lamp   **E.P.P.** Rear number plate lamp   **E.V.** Windscreen wiper   **F.1, F.2, F.4, F.5** 15 Amp fuses   **F.3** 8 Amp fuse   **F.S.** Parking lamp   **H.E.** Oil pressure and water temperature indicator   **I.A.D.** Starter switch   **I. Cli.** Flasher switch   **I.E.C.** Boot lamp switch   **I.E.V.** Windscreen wiper switch   **I.F.S.** Parking lamp switch   **I.P.** Door switch   **I.S.** Stop lamp switch   **J.R.** Fuel gauge   **J. Tr.** Fuel tank unit   **L.Ar.** Rear lamps   **L.Av.** Side lamps   **L.E.** Panel lamp   **M.C.A.** Brake warning light   **N.F.** Brake fluid level warning   **P.E.** Petrol pump   **Pr.** Headlamp   **Pr.H.** Spot lamp   **P.T.** Water temperature sender unit   **R** Horn relay   **R.bie** Battery master switch   **Reg** Regulator   **Rf.E.V.** Windscreen wash relay   **Rh.** Rheostat   **R.Pr.** Headlamp relay   **T.Cli** Flasher warning lamp   **T.H.** Oil pressure warning lamp   **Th.E.** Water thermometer   **Th.V.D.** Fan switch   **T.P.R.** Headlamp warning light   **Th.T.** Water temperature warning lamp   **V.D.** Electro-magnetic fan

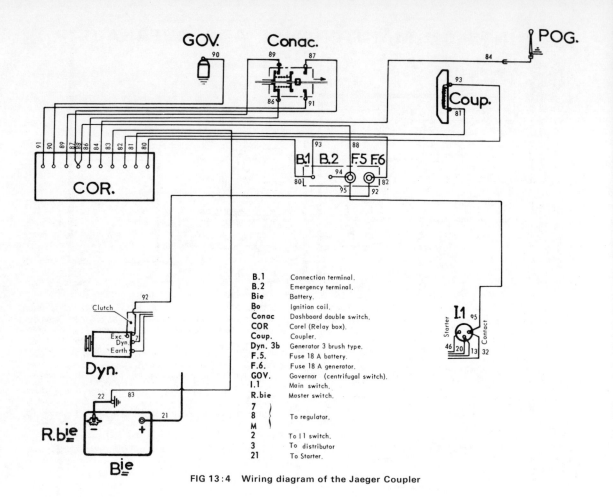

GOV.   Conac.   POG.

Coup.

COR.

B.1 B.2 F.5 F.6

Clutch

Exc.
Dyn.
Earth

Dyn.

R.bie

Bie

B.1	Connection terminal.
B.2	Emergency terminal.
Bie	Battery.
Bo	Ignition coil.
Conac	Dashboard double switch.
COR	Corel (Relay box).
Coup.	Coupler.
Dyn. 3b	Generator 3 brush type.
F.5.	Fuse 18 A battery.
F.6.	Fuse 18 A generator.
GOV.	Governor (centrifugal switch).
I.1	Main switch.
R.bie	Master switch.
7	
8	To regulator.
M	
2	To I1 switch.
3	To distributor.
21	To Starter.

FIG 13:4   Wiring diagram of the Jaeger Coupler

FIG 13:5   Timing adjustment check rod

HINTS ON MAINTENANCE AND OVERHAUL

There are few things more rewarding than the restoration of a vehicle's original peak of efficiency and smooth performance.

The following notes are intended to help the owner to reach that state of perfection. Providing that he possesses the basic manual skills he should have no difficulty in performing most of the operations detailed in this manual. It must be stressed, however, that where recommended in the manual, highly-skilled operations ought to be entrusted to experts, who have the necessary equipment, to carry out the work satisfactorily.

Quality of workmanship:

The hazardous driving conditions on the roads to-day demand that vehicles should be as nearly perfect, mechanically, as possible. It is therefore most important that amateur work be carried out with care, bearing in mind the often inadequate working conditions, and also the inferior tools which may have to be used. It is easy to counsel perfection in all things, and we recognize that it may be setting an impossibly high standard. We do, however, suggest that every care should be taken to ensure that a vehicle is as safe to take on the road as it is humanly possible to make it.

Safe working conditions:

Even though a vehicle may be stationary, it is still potentially dangerous if certain sensible precautions are not taken when working on it while it is supported on jacks or blocks. It is indeed preferable not to use jacks alone, but to supplement them with carefully placed blocks, so that there will be plenty of support if the car rolls off the jacks during a strenuous manoeuvre. Axle stands are an excellent way of providing a rigid base which is not readily disturbed. Piles of bricks are a dangerous substitute. Be careful not to get under heavy loads on lifting tackle, the load could fall. It is preferable not to work alone when lifting an engine, or when working underneath a vehicle which is supported well off the ground. To be trapped, particularly under the vehicle, may have unpleasant results if help is not quickly forthcoming. Make some provision, however humble, to deal with fires. Always disconnect a battery if there is a likelihood of electrical shorts. These may start a fire if there is leaking fuel about. This applies particularly to leads which can carry a heavy current, like those in the starter circuit. While on the subject of electricity, we must also stress the danger of using equipment which is run off the mains and which has no earth or has faulty wiring or connections. So many workshops have damp floors, and electrical shocks are of such a nature that it is sometimes impossible to let go of a live lead or piece of equipment due to the muscular spasms which take place.

Work demanding special care:

This involves the servicing of braking, steering and suspension systems. On the road, failure of the braking system may be disastrous. Make quite sure that there can be no possibility of failure through the bursting of rusty brake pipes or rotten hoses, nor to a sudden loss of pressure due to defective seals or valves.

Problems:

The chief problems which may face an operator are:
1 External dirt.
2 Difficulty in undoing tight fixings.
3 Dismantling unfamiliar mechanisms.
4 Deciding in what respect parts are defective.
5 Confusion about the correct order for reassembly.
6 Adjusting running clearances.
7 Road testing.
8 Final tuning.

Practical suggestion to solve the problems:

1 Preliminary cleaning of large parts—engines, transmissions, steering, suspensions, etc.,—should be carried out before removal from the car. Where road dirt and mud alone are present, wash clean with a high-pressure water jet, brushing to remove stubborn adhesions, and allow to drain and dry. Where oil or grease is also present, wash down with a proprietary compound (Gunk, Teepol etc.,) applying with a stiff brush—an old paint brush is suitable—into all crevices. Cover the distributor and ignition coils with a polythene bag and then apply a strong water jet to clear the loosened deposits. Allow to drain and dry. The assemblies will then be sufficiently clean to remove and transfer to the bench for the next stage.

On the bench, further cleaning can be carried out, first wiping the parts as free as possible from grease with old newspaper. Avoid using rag or cotton waste which can leave clogging fibres behind. Any remaining grease can be removed with a brush dipped in paraffin. If necessary, traces of paraffin can be removed by carbon tetrachloride. Avoid using paraffin or petrol in large quantities for cleaning in enclosed areas, such as garages, on account of the high fire risk.

When all exteriors have been cleaned, and not before, dismantling can be commenced. This ensures that dirt will not enter into interiors and orifices revealed by dismantling. In the next phases, where components have to be cleaned, use carbon tetrachloride in preference to petrol and keep the containers covered except when in use. After the components have been cleaned, plug small holes with tapered hard wood plugs cut to size and blank off larger orifices with greaseproof paper and masking tape. Do not use soft wood plugs or matchsticks as they may break.

2 It is not advisable to hammer on the end of a screw thread, but if it must be done, first screw on a nut to protect the thread, and use a lead hammer. This applies particularly to the removal of tapered cotters. Nuts and bolts seem to 'grow' together, especially in exhaust systems. If penetrating oil does not work, try the judicious application of heat, but be careful of starting a fire. Asbestos sheet or cloth is useful to isolate heat.

Tight bushes or pieces of tail-pipe rusted into a silencer can be removed by splitting them with an open-ended hacksaw. Tight screws can sometimes be started by a tap from a hammer on the end of a suitable screwdriver. Many tight fittings will yield to the judicious use of a hammer, but it must be a soft-faced hammer if damage is to be avoided, use a heavy block on the opposite side to absorb shock. Any parts of the steering system which have been damaged should be renewed, as attempts to repair them may lead to cracking and subsequent failure, and steering ball joints should be disconnected using a recommended tool to prevent damage.

3 If often happens that an owner is baffled when trying to dismantle an unfamiliar piece of equipment. So many modern devices are pressed together or assembled by spinning-over flanges, that they must be sawn apart. The intention is that the whole assembly must be renewed. However, parts which appear to be in one piece to the naked eye, may reveal close-fitting joint lines when inspected with a magnifying glass, and, this may provide the necessary clue to dismantling. Left-handed screw threads are used where rotational forces would tend to unscrew a right handed screw thread.

Be very careful when dismantling mechanisms which may come apart suddenly. Work in an enclosed space where the parts will be contained, and drape a piece of cloth over the device if springs are likely to fly in all directions. Mark everything which might be reassembled in the wrong position, scratched symbols may be used on unstressed parts, or a sequence of tiny dots from a centre punch can be useful. Stressed parts should never be scratched or centre-popped as this may lead to cracking under working conditions. Store parts which look alike in the correct order for reassembly. Never rely upon memory to assist in the assembly of complicated mechanisms, especially when they will be dismantled for a long time, but make notes, and drawings to supplement the diagrams in the manual, and put labels on detached wires. Rust stains may indicate unlubricated wear. This can sometimes be seen round the outside edge of a bearing cup in a universal joint. Look for bright rubbing marks on parts which normally should not make heavy contact. These might prove that something is bent or running out of truth. For example, there might be bright marks on one side of a piston, at the top near the ring grooves, and others at the bottom of the skirt on the other side. This could well be the clue to a bent connecting rod. Suspected cracks can be proved by heating the component in a light oil to approximately 100°C, removing, drying off, and dusting with french chalk, if a crack is present the oil retained in the crack will stain the french chalk.

4 In determining wear, and the degree, against the permissible limits set in the manual, accurate measurement can only be achieved by the use of a micrometer. In many cases, the wear is given to the fourth place of decimals; that is in ten-thousandths of an inch. This can be read by the vernier scale on the barrel of a good micrometer. Bore diameters are more difficult to determine. If, however, the matching shaft is accurately measured, the degree of play in the bore can be felt as a guide to its suitability. In other cases, the shank of a twist drill of known diameter is a handy check.

Many methods have been devised for determining the clearance between bearing surfaces. To-day the best and simplest is by the use of Plastigage, obtainable from most garages. A thin plastic thread is laid between the two surfaces and the bearing is tightened, flattening the thread. On removal, the width of the thread is compared with a scale supplied with the thread and the clearance is read off directly. Sometimes joint faces leak persistently, even after gasket renewal. The fault will then be traceable to distortion, dirt or burrs. Studs which are screwed into soft metal frequently raise burrs at the point of entry. A quick cure for this is to chamfer the edge of the hole in the part which fits over the stud.

5 **Always check a replacement part with the original one before it is fitted.**

If parts are not marked, and the order for reassembly is not known, a little detective work will help. Look for marks which are due to wear to see if they can be mated. Joint faces may not be identical due to manufacturing errors, and parts which overlap may be stained, giving a clue to the correct position. Most fixings leave identifying marks especially if they were painted over on assembly. It is then easier to decide whether a nut, for instance, has a plain, a spring, or a shakeproof washer under it. All running surfaces become 'bedded' together after long spells of work and tiny imperfections on one part will be found to have left corresponding marks on the other. This is particularly true of shafts and bearings and even a score on a cylinder wall will show on the piston.

6 Checking end float or rocker clearances by feeler gauge may not always give accurate results because of wear. For instance, the rocker tip which bears on a valve stem may be deeply pitted, in which case the feeler will simply be bridging a depression. Thrust washers may also wear depressions in opposing faces to make accurate measurement difficult. End float is then easier to check by using a dial gauge. It is common practice to adjust end play in bearing assemblies, like front hubs with taper rollers, by doing up the axle nut until the hub becomes stiff to turn and then backing it off a little. Do not use this method with ballbearing hubs as the assembly is often preloaded by tightening the axle nut to its fullest extent. If the splitpin hole will not line up, file the base of the nut a little.

Steering assemblies often wear in the straight-ahead position. If any part is adjusted, make sure that it remains free when moved from lock to lock. Do not be surprised if an assembly like a steering gearbox, which is known to be carefully adjusted outside the car, becomes stiff when it is bolted in place. This will be due to distortion of the case by the pull of the mounting bolts, particularly if the mounting points are not all touching together. This problem may be met in other equipment and is cured by careful attention to the alignment of mounting points.

When a spanner is stamped with a size and A/F it means that the dimension is the width between the jaws and has no connection with ANF, which is the designation for the American National Fine thread. Coarse threads like Whitworth are rarely used on cars to-day except for studs which screw into soft aluminium or cast iron. For this reason it might be found that the top end of a cylinder head stud has a fine thread and the lower end a coarse thread to screw into the cylinder block. If the car has mainly UNF threads then it is likely that any coarse threads will be UNC, which are not the same as Whitworth. Small sizes have the same number of threads in Whitworth and UNC, but in the $\frac{1}{2}$ inch size for example, there are twelve threads to the inch in the former and thirteen in the latter.

7 After a major overhaul, particularly if a great deal of work has been done on the braking, steering and suspension systems, it is advisable to approach the problem of testing with care. If the braking system has been overhauled, apply heavy pressure to the brake pedal and get a second operator to check every possible source of leakage. The brakes may work extremely well, but a leak could cause complete failure after a few miles.

Do not fit the hub caps until every wheel nut has been checked for tightness, and make sure the tyre pressures are correct. Check the levels of coolant, lubricants and hydraulic fluids. Being satisfied that all is well, take the car on the road and test the brakes at once. Check the steering and the action of the handbrake. Do all this at moderate speeds on quiet roads, and make sure there is no other vehicle behind you when you try a rapid stop.

Finally, remember that many parts settle down after a time, so check for tightness of all fixings after the car has been on the road for a hundred miles or so.

8 It is useless to tune an engine which has not reached its normal running temperature. In the same way, the tune of an engine which is stiff after a rebore will be different when the engine is again running free. Remember too, that rocker clearances on pushrod operated valve gear will change when the cylinder head nuts are tightened after an initial period of running with a new head gasket.

Trouble may not always be due to what seems the obvious cause. Ignition, carburation and mechanical condition are interdependent and spitting back through the carburetter, which might be attributed to a weak mixture, can be caused by a sticking inlet valve.

For one final hint on tuning, never adjust more than one thing at a time or it will be impossible to tell which adjustment produced the desired result.

Inches	Decimals	Milli-metres	Inches to Millimetres (Inches)	Inches to Millimetres (mm)	Millimetres to Inches (mm)	Millimetres to Inches (Inches)
1/64	.015625	.3969	.001	.0254	.01	.00039
1/32	.03125	.7937	.002	.0508	.02	.00079
3/64	.046875	1.1906	.003	.0762	.03	.00118
1/16	.0625	1.5875	.004	.1016	.04	.00157
5/64	.078125	1.9844	.005	.1270	.05	.00197
3/32	.09375	2.3812	.006	.1524	.06	.00236
7/64	.109375	2.7781	.007	.1778	.07	.00276
1/8	.125	3.1750	.008	.2032	.08	.00315
9/64	.140625	3.5719	.009	.2286	.09	.00354
5/32	.15625	3.9687	.01	.254	.1	.00394
11/64	.171875	4.3656	.02	.508	.2	.00787
3/16	.1875	4.7625	.03	.762	.3	.01181
13/64	.203125	5·1594	.04	1.016	.4	.01575
7/32	.21875	5.5562	.05	1.270	.5	.01969
15/64	.234375	5.9531	.06	1.524	.6	.02362
1/4	.25	6.3500	.07	1.778	.7	.02756
17/64	.265625	6.7469	.08	2.032	.8	.03150
9/32	.28125	7.1437	.09	2.286	.9	.03543
19/64	.296875	7.5406	.1	2.54	1	.03937
5/16	.3125	7.9375	.2	5.08	2	.07874
21/64	.328125	8.3344	.3	7.62	3	.11811
11/32	.34375	8.7312	.4	10.16	4	.15748
23/64	.359375	9.1281	.5	12.70	5	.19685
3/8	.375	9.5250	.6	15.24	6	.23622
25/64	.390625	9.9219	.7	17.78	7	.27559
13/32	.40625	10.3187	.8	20.32	8	.31496
27/64	.421875	10.7156	.9	22.86	9	.35433
7/16	.4375	11.1125	1	25.4	10	.39370
29/64	.453125	11.5094	2	50.8	11	.43307
15/32	.46875	11.9062	3	76.2	12	.47244
31/64	.484375	12.3031	4	101.6	13	.51181
1/2	.5	12.7000	5	127.0	14	.55118
33/64	.515625	13.0969	6	152.4	15	.59055
17/32	.53125	13.4937	7	177.8	16	.62992
35/64	.546875	13.8906	8	203.2	17	.66929
9/16	.5625	14.2875	9	228.6	18	.70866
37/64	.578125	14.6844	10	254.0	19	.74803
19/32	.59375	15.0812	11	279.4	20	.78740
39/64	.609375	15.4781	12	304.8	21	.82677
5/8	.625	15.8750	13	330.2	22	.86614
41/64	.640625	16.2719	14	355.6	23	.90551
21/32	.65625	16.6687	15	381.0	24	.94488
43/64	.671875	17.0656	16	406.4	25	.98425
11/16	.6875	17.4625	17	431.8	26	1.02362
45/64	.703125	17.8594	18	457.2	27	1.06299
23/32	.71875	18.2562	19	482.6	28	1.10236
47/64	.734375	18.6531	20	508.0	29	1.14173
3/4	.75	19.0500	21	533.4	30	1.18110
49/64	.765625	19.4469	22	558.8	31	1.22047
25/32	.78125	19.8437	23	584.2	32	1.25984
51/64	.796875	20.2406	24	609.6	33	1.29921
13/16	.8125	20.6375	25	635.0	34	1.33858
53/64	.828125	21.0344	26	660.4	35	1.37795
27/32	.84375	21.4312	27	685.8	36	1.41732
55/64	.859375	21.8281	28	711.2	37	1.4567
7/8	.875	22.2250	29	736.6	38	1.4961
57/64	.890625	22.6219	30	762.0	39	1.5354
29/32	.90625	23.0187	31	787.4	40	1.5748
59/64	.921875	23.4156	32	812.8	41	1.6142
15/16	.9375	23.8125	33	838.2	42	1.6535
61/64	.953125	24.2094	34	863.6	43	1.6929
31/32	.96875	24.6062	35	889.0	44	1.7323
63/64	.984375	25.0031	36	914.4	45	1.7717

UNITS	Pints to Litres	Gallons to Litres	Litres to Pints	Litres to Gallons	Miles to Kilometres	Kilometres to Miles	Lbs. per sq. In. to Kg. per sq. Cm.	Kg. per sq. Cm. to Lbs. per sq. In.
1	.57	4.55	1.76	.22	1.61	.62	.07	14.22
2	1.14	9.09	3.52	.44	3.22	1.24	.14	28.50
3	1.70	13.64	5.28	.66	4.83	1.86	.21	42.67
4	2.27	18.18	7.04	.88	6.44	2.49	.28	56.89
5	2.84	22.73	8.80	1.10	8.05	3.11	.35	71.12
6	3.41	27.28	10.56	1.32	9.66	3.73	.42	85.34
7	3.98	31.82	12.32	1.54	11.27	4.35	.49	99.56
8	4.55	36.37	14.08	1.76	12.88	4.97	.56	113.79
9		40.91	15.84	1.98	14.48	5.59	.63	128.00
10		45.46	17.60	2.20	16.09	6.21	.70	142.23
20				4.40	32.19	12.43	1.41	284.47
30				6.60	48.28	18.64	2.11	426.70
40				8.80	64.37	24.85		
50					80.47	31.07		
60					96.56	37.28		
70					112.65	43.50		
80					128.75	49.71		
90					144.84	55.92		
100					160.93	62.14		

UNITS	Lb ft to kgm	Kgm to lb ft	UNITS	Lb ft to kgm	Kgm to lb ft
1	.138	7.233	7	.967	50.631
2	.276	14.466	8	1.106	57.864
3	.414	21.699	9	1.244	65.097
4	.553	28.932	10	1.382	72.330
5	.691	36.165	20	2.765	144.660
6	.829	43.398	30	4.147	216.990

GLOSSARY OF TERMS

Allen key   Cranked wrench of hexagonal section for use with socket head screws.

Alternator   Electrical generator producing alternating current. Rectified to direct current for battery charging.

Ambient temperature   Surrounding atmospheric temperature.

Annulus   Used in engineering to indicate the outer ring gear of an epicyclic gear train.

Armature   The shaft carrying the windings, which rotates in the magnetic field of a generator or starter motor. That part of a solenoid or relay which is activated by the magnetic field.

Axial   In line with, or pertaining to, an axis.

Backlash   Play in meshing gears.

Balance lever   A bar where force applied at the centre is equally divided between connections at the ends.

Banjo axle   Axle casing with large diameter housing for the crownwheel and differential.

Bendix pinion   A self-engaging and self-disengaging drive on a starter motor shaft.

Bevel pinion   A conical shaped gearwheel, designed to mesh with a similar gear with an axis usually at 90 deg. to its own.

bhp   Brake horse power, measured on a dynamometer.

bmep   Brake mean effective pressure. Average pressure on a piston during the working stroke.

Brake cylinder   Cylinder with hydraulically operated piston(s) acting on brake shoes or pad(s).

Brake regulator   Control valve fitted in hydraulic braking system which limits brake pressure to rear brakes during heavy braking to prevent rear wheel locking.

Camber   Angle at which a wheel is tilted from the vertical.

Capacitor   Modern term for an electrical condenser. Part of distributor assembly, connected across contact breaker points, acts as an interference suppressor.

Castellated   Top face of a nut, slotted across the flats, to take a locking splitpin.

Castor   Angle at which the kingpin or swivel pin is tilted when viewed from the side.

cc   Cubic centimetres. Engine capacity is arrived at by multiplying the area of the bore in sq cm by the stroke in cm by the number of cylinders.

Clevis   U-shaped forked connector used with a clevis pin, usually at handbrake connections.

Collet   A type of collar, usually split and located in a groove in a shaft, and held in place by a retainer. The arrangement used to retain the spring(s) on a valve stem in most cases.

Commutator   Rotating segmented current distributor between armature windings and brushes in generator or motor.

Compression ratio   The ratio, or quantitative relation, of the total volume (piston at bottom of stroke) to the unswept volume (piston at top of stroke) in an engine cylinder.

Condenser   See capacitor.

Core plug   Plug for blanking off a manufacturing hole in a casting.

Crownwheel   Large bevel gear in rear axle, driven by a bevel pinion attached to the propeller shaft. Sometimes called a 'ring gear'.

'C'-spanner   Like a 'C' with a handle. For use on screwed collars without flats, but with slots or holes.

Damper   Modern term for shock-absorber, used in vehicle suspension systems to damp out spring oscillations.

Depression   The lowering of atmospheric pressure as in the inlet manifold and carburetter.

Dowel   Close tolerance pin, peg, tube, or bolt, which accurately locates mating parts.

Drag link   Rod connecting steering box drop arm (pitman arm) to nearest front wheel steering arm in certain types of steering systems.

Dry liner   Thinwall tube pressed into cylinder bore

Dry sump   Lubrication system where all oil is scavenged from the sump, and returned to a separate tank.

Dynamo   See Generator.

Electrode   Terminal, part of an electrical component, such as the points or 'Electrodes' of a sparking plug.

Electrolyte   In lead-acid car batteries a solution of sulphuric acid and distilled water.

End float   The axial movement between associated parts, end play.

EP   Extreme pressure. In lubricants, special grades for heavily loaded bearing surfaces, such as gear teeth in a gearbox, or crownwheel and pinion in a rear axle.

Fade	Of brakes. Reduced efficiency due to overheating.
Field coils	Windings on the polepieces of motors and generators.
Fillets	Narrow finishing strips usually applied to interior bodywork.
First motion shaft	Input shaft from clutch to gearbox.
Fullflow filter	Filters in which all the oil is pumped to the engine. If the element becomes clogged, a bypass valve operates to pass unfiltered oil to the engine.
FWD	Front wheel drive.
Gear pump	Two meshing gears in a close fitting casing. Oil is carried from the inlet round the outside of both gears in the spaces between the gear teeth and casing to the outlet, the meshing gear teeth prevent oil passing back to the inlet, and the oil is forced through the outlet port.
Generator	Modern term for 'Dynamo'. When rotated produces electrical current.
Grommet	A ring of protective or sealing material. Can be used to protect pipes or leads passing through bulkheads.
Grubscrew	Fully threaded headless screw with screwdriver slot. Used for locking, or alignment purposes.
Gudgeon pin	Shaft which connects a piston to its connecting rod. Sometimes called 'wrist pin', or 'piston pin'.
Halfshaft	One of a pair transmitting drive from the differential.
Helical	In spiral form. The teeth of helical gears are cut at a spiral angle to the side faces of the gearwheel.
Hot spot	Hot area that assists vapourisation of fuel on its way to cylinders. Often provided by close contact between inlet and exhaust manifolds.
HT	High Tension. Applied to electrical current produced by the ignition coil for the sparking plugs.
Hydrometer	A device for checking specific gravity of liquids. Used to check specific gravity of electrolyte.
Hypoid bevel gears	A form of bevel gear used in the rear axle drive gears. The bevel pinion meshes below the centre line of the crownwheel, giving a lower propeller shaft line.
Idler	A device for passing on movement. A free running gear between driving and driven gears. A lever transmitting track rod movement to a side rod in steering gear.
Impeller	A centrifugal pumping element. Used in water pumps to stimulate flow.

Journals	Those parts of a shaft that are in contact with the bearings.
Kingpin	The main vertical pin which carries the front wheel spindle, and permits steering movement. May be called 'steering pin' or 'swivel pin'.
Layshaft	The shaft which carries the laygear in the gearbox. The laygear is driven by the first motion shaft and drives the third motion shaft according to the gear selected. Sometimes called the 'countershaft' or 'second motion shaft.'
lb ft	A measure of twist or torque. A pull of 10 lb at a radius of 1 ft is a torque of 10 lb ft.
lb/sq in	Pounds per square inch.
Little-end	The small, or piston end of a connecting rod. Sometimes called the 'small-end'.
LT	Low Tension. The current output from the battery.
Mandrel	Accurately manufactured bar or rod used for test or centring purposes.
Manifold	A pipe, duct, or chamber, with several branches.
Needle rollers	Bearing rollers with a length many times their diameter.
Oil bath	Reservoir which lubricates parts by immersion. In air filters, a separate oil supply for wetting a wire mesh element to hold the dust.
Oil wetted	In air filters, a wire mesh element lightly oiled to trap and hold airborne dust.
Overlap	Period during which inlet and exhaust valves are open together.
Panhard rod	Bar connected between fixed point on chassis and another on axle to control sideways movement.
Pawl	Pivoted catch which engages in the teeth of a ratchet to permit movement in one direction only.
Peg spanner	Tool with pegs, or pins, to engage in holes or slots in the part to be turned.
Pendant pedals	Pedals with levers that are pivoted at the top end.
Phillips screwdriver	A cross-point screwdriver for use with the cross-slotted heads of Phillips screws.
Pinion	A small gear, usually in relation to another gear.
Piston-type damper	Shock absorber in which damping is controlled by a piston working in a closed oil-filled cylinder.
Preloading	Preset static pressure on ball or roller bearings not due to working loads.
Radial	Radiating from a centre, like the spokes of a wheel.

Radius rod	Pivoted arm confining movement of a part to an arc of fixed radius.
Ratchet	Toothed wheel or rack which can move in one direction only, movement in the other being prevented by a pawl.
Ring gear	A gear tooth ring attached to outer periphery of flywheel. Starter pinion engages with it during starting.
Runout	Amount by which rotating part is out of true.
Semi-floating axle	Outer end of rear axle halfshaft is carried on bearing inside axle casing. Wheel hub is secured to end of shaft.
Servo	A hydraulic or pneumatic system for assisting, or, augmenting a physical effort. See 'Vacuum Servo'.
Setscrew	One which is threaded for the full length of the shank.
Shackle	A coupling link, used in the form of two parallel pins connected by side plates to secure the end of the master suspension spring and absorb the effects of deflection.
Shell bearing	Thinwalled steel shell lined with anti-friction metal. Usually semi-circular and used in pairs for main and big-end bearings.
Shock absorber	See 'Damper'.
Silentbloc	Rubber bush bonded to inner and outer metal sleeves.
Socket-head screw	Screw with hexagonal socket for an Allen key.
Solenoid	A coil of wire creating a magnetic field when electric current passes through it. Used with a soft iron core to operate contacts or a mechanical device.
Spur gear	A gear with teeth cut axially across the periphery.
Stub axle	Short axle fixed at one end only.
Tachometer	An instrument for accurate measurement of rotating speed. Usually indicates in revolutions per minute.

TDC	Top Dead Centre. The highest point reached by a piston in a cylinder, with the crank and connecting rod in line.
Thermostat	Automatic device for regulating temperature. Used in vehicle coolant systems to open a valve which restricts circulation at low temperature.
Third motion shaft	Output shaft of gearbox.
Threequarter floating axle	Outer end of rear axle halfshaft flanged and bolted to wheel hub, which runs on bearing mounted on outside of axle casing. Vehicle weight is not carried by the axle shaft.
Thrust bearing or washer	Used to reduce friction in rotating parts subject to axial loads.
Torque	Turning or twisting effort. See 'lb ft'.
Track rod	The bar(s) across the vehicle which connect the steering arms and maintain the front wheels in their correct alignment.
UJ	Universal joint. A coupling between shafts which permits angular movement.
UNF	Unified National Fine screw thread.
Vacuum servo	Device used in brake system, using difference between atmospheric pressure and inlet manifold depression to operate a piston which acts to augment brake pressure as required. See 'Servo'.
Venturi	A restriction or 'choke' in a tube, as in a carburetter, used to increase velocity to obtain a reduction in pressure.
Vernier	A sliding scale for obtaining fractional readings of the graduations of an adjacent scale.
Welch plug	A domed thin metal disc which is partially flattened to lock in a recess. Used to plug core holes in castings.
Wet liner	Removable cylinder barrel, sealed against coolant leakage, where the coolant is in direct contact with the outer surface.
Wet sump	A reservoir attached to the crankcase to hold the lubricating oil.

NOTES

INDEX

Alfa Romeo Giulia 1600,
1750, 2000 1960 on
Aston Martin 1921-58
Auto Union Audi 70, 80,
Super 90, 1966-72
Audi 100 1969 on
Austin, Morris etc.
1100 Mk. 1 1962-67
Austin, Morris etc. 1100
Mk. 2, 3, 1300 Mk. 1, 2, 3
America 1968 on
Austin A30, A35, A40
Farina 1951-67
Austin A55 Mk. 2, A60
1958-69
Austin A99, A110 1959-68
Austin J4 1960 on
Austin Allegro 1973 on
Austin Maxi 1969 on
Austin, Morris 1800
1964 on
Austin, Morris 2200 1972 on
Austin Kimberley, Tasman
1970 on
Austin, Morris 1300, 1500
Nomad 1969 on
BMC 3 (Austin A50, A55
Mk. 1, Morris Oxford
2, 3 1954-59)
Austin Healey 100/6,
3000 1956-68
Austin Healey, MG
Sprite, Midget 1958 on
Bedford CA Mk. 2 1964-69
Bedford CF Vans 1969 on
Bedford Beagle HA Vans
1964 on
BMW 1600 1966 on
BMW 1800 1964-71
BMW 2000, 2002 1966 on
Chevrolet Corvair 1960-69
Chevrolet Corvette V8
1957-65
Chevrolet Corvette V8
1965 on
Chevrolet Vega 2300
1970 on
Chrysler Valiant V8
1965 on
Chrysler Valiant Straight
Six 1963 on
Citroen DS 19, ID 19
1955-66
Citroen ID 19, DS 19, 20,
21 1966 on
Citroen Dyane Ami 1964 on
Daf 31, 32, 33, 44, 55
1961 on
Datsun Bluebird 610 series
1972 on
Datsun Cherry 100A, 120A
1971 on
Datsun 1000, 1200 1968 on
Datsun 1300, 1400, 1600
1968 on
Datsun 240C 1971 on

Datsun 240Z Sport 1970 on
Fiat 124 1966 on
Fiat 124 Sport 1966 on
Fiat 125 1967-72
Fiat 127 1971 on
Fiat 128 1969 on
Fiat 500 1957 on
Fiat 600, 600D 1955-69
Fiat 850 1964 on
Fiat 1100 1957-69
Fiat 1300, 1500 1961-67
Ford Anglia Prefect 100E
1953-62
Ford Anglia 105E, Prefect
107E 1959-67
Ford Capri 1300, 1600 OHV
1968 on
Ford Capri 1300, 1600,
2000 OHC 1972 on
Ford Capri 2000 V4, 3000 V6
1969 on
Ford Classic, Capri
1961-64
Ford Consul, Zephyr,
Zodiac, 1, 2 1950-62
Ford Corsair Straight
Four 1963-65
Ford Corsair V4 1965-68
Ford Corsair V4 2000
1969-70
Ford Cortina 1962-66
Ford Cortina 1967-68
Ford Cortina 1969-70
Ford Cortina Mk. 3
1970 on
Ford Escort 1967 on
Ford Falcon 6 1964-70
Ford Falcon XK, XL
1960-63
Ford Falcon 6 XR/XA
1966 on
Ford Falcon V8 (U.S.A.)
1965-71
Ford Falcon V8 (Aust.)
1966 on
Ford Pinto 1970 on
Ford Maverick 6 1969 on
Ford Maverick V8 1970 on
Ford Mustang 6 1965 on
Ford Mustang V8 1965 on
Ford Thames 10, 12,
15 cwt 1957-65
Ford Transit V4 1965 on
Ford Zephyr Zodiac Mk. 3
1962-66
Ford Zephyr Zodiac V4,
V6, Mk. 4 1966-72
Ford Consul, Granada
1972 on
Hillman Avenger 1970 on
Hillman Hunter 1966 on
Hillman Imp 1963-68
Hillman Imp 1969 on
Hillman Minx 1 to 5
1956-65
Hillman Minx 1965-67

Hillman Minx 1966-70
Hillman Super Minx
1961-65
Jaguar XK120, 140, 150,
Mk. 7, 8, 9 1948-61
Jaguar 2.4, 3.4, 3.8 Mk.
1, 2 1955-69
Jaguar 'E' Type 1961-72
Jaguar 'S' Type 420
1963-68
Jaguar XJ6 1968 on
Jowett Javelin Jupiter
1947-53
Landrover 1, 2 1948-61
Landrover 2, 2a, 3 1959 on
Mazda 616 1970 on
Mazda 808, 818 1972 on
Mazda 1200, 1300 1969 on
Mazda 1500, 1800 1967 on
Mazda RX-2 1971 on
Mazda R100, RX-3 1970 on
Mercedes-Benz 190b,
190c, 200 1959-68
Mercedes-Benz 220
1959-65
Mercedes-Benz 220/8
1968 on
Mercedes-Benz 230
1963-68
Mercedes-Benz 250
1965-67
Mercedes-Benz 250
1968 on
Mercedes-Benz 280
1968 on
MG TA to TF 1936-55
MGA MGB 1955-68
MGB 1969 on
Mini 1959 on
Mini Cooper 1961-72
Morgan Four 1936-72
Morris Marina 1971 on
Morris (Aust) Marina
1972 on
Morris Minor 2, 1000
1952-71
Morris Oxford 5, 6 1959-71
NSU 1000 1963-72
NSU Prinz 1 to 4 1957-72
Opel Ascona, Manta
1970 on
Opel GT 1900 1968 on
Opel Kadett, Olympia 993 cc
1078 cc 1962 on
Opel Kadett, Olympia 1492,
1698, 1897 cc 1967 on
Opel Rekord C 1966-72
Peugeot 204 1965 on
Peugeot 304 1970 on
Peugeot 404 1960 on
Peugeot 504 1968 on
Porsche 356A, B, C 1957-65
Porsche 911 1964 on
Porsche 912 1965-69
Porsche 914 S 1969 on
Reliant Regal 1952-73

Renault R4, R4L, 4 1961 on
Renault 5 1972 on
Renault 6 1968 on
Renault 8, 10, 1100 1962-71
Renault 12, 1969 on
Renault 15, 17 1971 on
Renault R16 1965 on
Renault Dauphine
Floride 1957-67
Renault Caravelle 1962-68
Rover 60 to 110 1953-64
Rover 2000 1963-73
Rover 3 Litre 1958-67
Rover 3500, 3500S 1968 on

Saab 95, 96, Sport
1960-68
Saab 99 1969 on
Saab V4 1966 on
Simca 1000 1961 on
Simca 1100 1967 on
Simca 1300, 1301, 1500,
1501 1963 on
Skoda One (440, 445, 450)
1955-70
Sunbeam Rapier Alpine
1955-65

Toyota Carina, Celica
1971 on
Toyota Corolla 1100,
1200 1967 on
Toyota Corona 1500 Mk. 1
1965-70
Toyota Corona Mk. 2
1969 on
Triumph TR2, TR3, TR3A
1952-62
Triumph TR4, TR4A
1961-67
Triumph TR5, TR250,
TR6 1967 on
Triumph 1300, 1500
1965-73
Triumph 2000 Mk. 1, 2.5 PI
Mk. 1 1963-69
Triumph 2000 Mk. 2, 2.5 PI
Mk. 2 1969 on
Triumph Dolomite 1972 on
Triumph Herald 1959-68
Triumph Herald 1969-71
Triumph Spitfire, Vitesse
1962-68
Triumph Spitfire Mk. 3, 4
1969 on
Triumph GT6, Vitesse
2 Litre 1969 on
Triumph Stag 1970 on
Triumph Toledo 1970 on

Vauxhall Velox, Cresta
1957-72
Vauxhall Victor 1, 2, FB
1957-64
Vauxhall Victor 101
1964-67
Vauxhall Victor FD 1600,
2000 1967-72

Continued on following page

Vauxhall Victor 3300,
Ventora 1968-72
Vauxhall Victor FE
Ventora 1972 on
Vauxhall Viva HA 1963-66
Vauxhall Viva HB 1966-70

Vauxhall Viva, HC Firenza
1971 on
Volkswagen Beetle 1954-67
Volkswagen Beetle 1968 on
Volkswagen 1500 1961-66

Volkswagen 1600 Fastback
1965-73
Volkswagen Transporter
1954-67
Volkswagen Transporter
1968 on

Volkswagen 411 1968-72
Volvo 120 series 1961-70
Volvo 140 series 1966 on
Volvo 160 series 1968 on
Volvo 1800 1960-73